Mometrix
TEST PREPARATION

MCA

Success Strategies Grade 10 Reading

I0894312

DEAR FUTURE EXAM SUCCESS STORY

First of all, **THANK YOU** for purchasing Mometrix study materials!

Second, congratulations! You are one of the few determined test-takers who are committed to doing whatever it takes to excel on your exam. **You have come to the right place.** We developed these study materials with one goal in mind: to deliver you the information you need in a format that's concise and easy to use.

In addition to optimizing your guide for the content of the test, we've outlined our recommended steps for breaking down the preparation process into small, attainable goals so you can make sure you stay on track.

We've also analyzed the entire test-taking process, identifying the most common pitfalls and showing how you can overcome them and be ready for any curveball the test throws you.

Standardized testing is one of the biggest obstacles on your road to success, which only increases the importance of doing well in the high-pressure, high-stakes environment of test day. Your results on this test could have a significant impact on your future, and this guide provides the information and practical advice to help you achieve your full potential on test day.

Your success is our success

We would love to hear from you! If you would like to share the story of your exam success or if you have any questions or comments in regard to our products, please contact us at **800-673-8175** or **support@mometrix.com**.

Thanks again for your business and we wish you continued success!

Sincerely,
The Mometrix Test Preparation Team

Written and edited by the Mometrix Test Preparation Team
Printed in the United States of America

TABLE OF CONTENTS

Introduction

Thank you for purchasing this resource! You have made the choice to prepare yourself for a test that could have a huge impact on your future, and this guide is designed to help you be fully ready for test day. Obviously, it's important to have a solid understanding of the test material, but you also need to be prepared for the unique environment and stressors of the test, so that you can perform to the best of your abilities.

For this purpose, the first section that appears in this guide is the **Success Strategies**. We've devoted countless hours to meticulously researching what works and what doesn't, and we've boiled down our findings to the most impactful steps you can take to improve your performance on the test. We start at the beginning with study planning and move through the preparation process, all the way to the testing strategies that will help you get the most out of what you know when you're finally sitting in front of the test.

We recommend that you start preparing for your test as far in advance as possible. However, if you've bought this guide as a last-minute study resource and only have a few days before your test, we recommend that you skip over the first two Success Strategies since they address a long-term study plan.

If you struggle with **test anxiety**, we strongly encourage you to check out our recommendations for how you can overcome it. Test anxiety is a formidable foe, but it can be beaten, and we want to make sure you have the tools you need to defeat it.

Strategy #1 – Plan Big, Study Small

There's a lot riding on your performance. If you want to ace this test, you're going to need to keep your skills sharp and the material fresh in your mind. You need a plan that lets you review everything you need to know while still fitting in your schedule. We'll break this strategy down into three categories.

Information Organization

Start with the information you already have: the official test outline. From this, you can make a complete list of all the concepts you need to cover before the test. Organize these concepts into groups that can be studied together, and create a list of any related vocabulary you need to learn so you can brush up on any difficult terms. You'll want to keep this vocabulary list handy once you actually start studying since you may need to add to it along the way.

Time Management

Once you have your set of study concepts, decide how to spread them out over the time you have left before the test. Break your study plan into small, clear goals so you have a manageable task for each day and know exactly what you're doing. Then just focus on one small step at a time. When you manage your time this way, you don't need to spend hours at a time studying. Studying a small block of content for a short period each day helps you retain information better and avoid stressing over how much you have left to do. You can relax knowing that you have a plan to cover everything in time. In order for this strategy to be effective though, you have to start studying early and stick to your schedule. Avoid the exhaustion and futility that comes from last-minute cramming!

Study Environment

The environment you study in has a big impact on your learning. Studying in a coffee shop, while probably more enjoyable, is not likely to be as fruitful as studying in a quiet room. It's important to keep distractions to a minimum. You're only planning to study for a short block of time, so make the most of it. Don't pause to check your phone or get up to find a snack. It's also important to **avoid multitasking**. Research has consistently shown that multitasking will make your studying dramatically less effective. Your study area should also be comfortable and well-lit so you don't have the distraction of straining your eyes or sitting on an uncomfortable chair.

The time of day you study is also important. You want to be rested and alert. Don't wait until just before bedtime. Study when you'll be most likely to comprehend and remember. Even better, if you know what time of day your test will be, set that time aside for study. That way your brain will be used to working on that subject at that specific time and you'll have a better chance of recalling information.

Finally, it can be helpful to team up with others who are studying for the same test. Your actual studying should be done in as isolated an environment as possible, but the work of organizing the information and setting up the study plan can be divided up. In between study sessions, you can discuss with your teammates the concepts that you're all studying and quiz each other on the details. Just be sure that your teammates are as serious about the test as you are. If you find that your study time is being replaced with social time, you might need to find a new team.

Strategy #2 – Make Your Studying Count

You're devoting a lot of time and effort to preparing for this test, so you want to be absolutely certain it will pay off. This means doing more than just reading the content and hoping you can remember it on test day. It's important to make every minute of study count. There are two main areas you can focus on to make your studying count.

Retention

It doesn't matter how much time you study if you can't remember the material. You need to make sure you are retaining the concepts. To check your retention of the information you're learning, try recalling it at later times with minimal prompting. Try carrying around flashcards and glance at one or two from time to time or ask a friend who's also studying for the test to quiz you.

To enhance your retention, look for ways to put the information into practice so that you can apply it rather than simply recalling it. If you're using the information in practical ways, it will be much easier to remember. Similarly, it helps to solidify a concept in your mind if you're not only reading it to yourself but also explaining it to someone else. Ask a friend to let you teach them about a concept you're a little shaky on (or speak aloud to an imaginary audience if necessary). As you try to summarize, define, give examples, and answer your friend's questions, you'll understand the concepts better and they will stay with you longer. Finally, step back for a big picture view and ask yourself how each piece of information fits with the whole subject. When you link the different concepts together and see them working together as a whole, it's easier to remember the individual components.

Finally, practice showing your work on any multi-step problems, even if you're just studying. Writing out each step you take to solve a problem will help solidify the process in your mind, and you'll be more likely to remember it during the test.

Modality

Modality simply refers to the means or method by which you study. Choosing a study modality that fits your own individual learning style is crucial. No two people learn best in exactly the same way, so it's important to know your strengths and use them to your advantage.

For example, if you learn best by visualization, focus on visualizing a concept in your mind and draw an image or a diagram. Try color-coding your notes, illustrating them, or creating symbols that will trigger your mind to recall a learned concept. If you learn best by hearing or discussing information, find a study partner who learns the same way or read aloud to yourself. Think about how to put the information in your own words. Imagine that you are giving a lecture on the topic and record yourself so you can listen to it later.

For any learning style, flashcards can be helpful. Organize the information so you can take advantage of spare moments to review. Underline key words or phrases. Use different colors for different categories. Mnemonic devices (such as creating a short list in which every item starts with the same letter) can also help with retention. Find what works best for you and use it to store the information in your mind most effectively and easily.

Strategy #3 – Practice the Right Way

Your success on test day depends not only on how many hours you put into preparing, but also on whether you prepared the right way. It's good to check along the way to see if your studying is paying off. One of the most effective ways to do this is by taking practice tests to evaluate your progress. Practice tests are useful because they show exactly where you need to improve. Every time you take a practice test, pay special attention to these three groups of questions:

- The questions you got wrong
- The questions you had to guess on, even if you guessed right
- The questions you found difficult or slow to work through

This will show you exactly what your weak areas are, and where you need to devote more study time. Ask yourself why each of these questions gave you trouble. Was it because you didn't understand the material? Was it because you didn't remember the vocabulary? Do you need more repetitions on this type of question to build speed and confidence? Dig into those questions and figure out how you can strengthen your weak areas as you go back to review the material.

Additionally, many practice tests have a section explaining the answer choices. It can be tempting to read the explanation and think that you now have a good understanding of the concept. However, an explanation likely only covers part of the question's broader context. Even if the explanation makes perfect sense, **go back and investigate** every concept related to the question until you're positive you have a thorough understanding.

As you go along, keep in mind that the practice test is just that: practice. Memorizing these questions and answers will not be very helpful on the actual test because it is unlikely to have any of the same exact questions. If you only know the right answers to the sample questions, you won't be prepared for the real thing. **Study the concepts** until you understand them fully, and then you'll be able to answer any question that shows up on the test.

It's important to wait on the practice tests until you're ready. If you take a test on your first day of study, you may be overwhelmed by the amount of material covered and how much you need to learn. Work up to it gradually.

On test day, you'll need to be prepared for answering questions, managing your time, and using the test-taking strategies you've learned. It's a lot to balance, like a mental marathon that will have a big impact on your future. Like training for a marathon, you'll need to start slowly and work your way up. When test day arrives, you'll be ready.

Start with the strategies you've read in the first two Success Strategies—plan your course and study in the way that works best for you. If you have time, consider using multiple study resources to get different approaches to the same concepts. It can be helpful to see difficult concepts from more than one angle. Then find a good source for practice tests. Many times, the test website will suggest potential study resources or provide sample tests.

Practice Test Strategy

If you're able to find at least three practice tests, we recommend this strategy:

UNTIMED AND OPEN-BOOK PRACTICE

Take the first test with no time constraints and with your notes and study guide handy. Take your time and focus on applying the strategies you've learned.

TIMED AND OPEN-BOOK PRACTICE

Take the second practice test open-book as well, but set a timer and practice pacing yourself to finish in time.

TIMED AND CLOSED-BOOK PRACTICE

Take any other practice tests as if it were test day. Set a timer and put away your study materials. Sit at a table or desk in a quiet room, imagine yourself at the testing center, and answer questions as quickly and accurately as possible.

Keep repeating timed and closed-book tests on a regular basis until you run out of practice tests or it's time for the actual test. Your mind will be ready for the schedule and stress of test day, and you'll be able to focus on recalling the material you've learned.

Strategy #4 – Pace Yourself

Once you're fully prepared for the material on the test, your biggest challenge on test day will be managing your time. Just knowing that the clock is ticking can make you panic even if you have plenty of time left. Work on pacing yourself so you can build confidence against the time constraints of the exam. Pacing is a difficult skill to master, especially in a high-pressure environment, so **practice is vital.**

Set time expectations for your pace based on how much time is available. For example, if a section has 60 questions and the time limit is 30 minutes, you know you have to average 30 seconds or less per question in order to answer them all. Although 30 seconds is the hard limit, set 25 seconds per question as your goal, so you reserve extra time to spend on harder questions. When you budget extra time for the harder questions, you no longer have any reason to stress when those questions take longer to answer.

Don't let this time expectation distract you from working through the test at a calm, steady pace, but keep it in mind so you don't spend too much time on any one question. Recognize that taking extra time on one question you don't understand may keep you from answering two that you do understand later in the test. If your time limit for a question is up and you're still not sure of the answer, mark it and move on, and come back to it later if the time and the test format allow. If the testing format doesn't allow you to return to earlier questions, just make an educated guess; then put it out of your mind and move on.

On the easier questions, be careful not to rush. It may seem wise to hurry through them so you have more time for the challenging ones, but it's not worth missing one if you know the concept and just didn't take the time to read the question fully. Work efficiently but make sure you understand the question and have looked at all of the answer choices, since more than one may seem right at first.

Even if you're paying attention to the time, you may find yourself a little behind at some point. You should speed up to get back on track, but do so wisely. Don't panic; just take a few seconds less on each question until you're caught up. Don't guess without thinking, but do look through the answer choices and eliminate any you know are wrong. If you can get down to two choices, it is often worthwhile to guess from those. Once you've chosen an answer, move on and don't dwell on any that you skipped or had to hurry through. If a question was taking too long, chances are it was one of the harder ones, so you weren't as likely to get it right anyway.

On the other hand, if you find yourself getting ahead of schedule, it may be beneficial to slow down a little. The more quickly you work, the more likely you are to make a careless mistake that will affect your score. You've budgeted time for each question, so don't be afraid to spend that time. Practice an efficient but careful pace to get the most out of the time you have.

Test-Taking Strategies

This section contains a list of test-taking strategies that you may find helpful as you work through the test. By taking what you know and applying logical thought, you can maximize your chances of answering any question correctly!

It is very important to realize that every question is different and every person is different: no single strategy will work on every question, and no single strategy will work for every person. That's why we've included all of them here, so you can try them out and determine which ones work best for different types of questions and which ones work best for you.

Question Strategies

⊘ Read Carefully

Read the question and the answer choices carefully. Don't miss the question because you misread the terms. You have plenty of time to read each question thoroughly and make sure you understand what is being asked. Yet a happy medium must be attained, so don't waste too much time. You must read carefully and efficiently.

⊘ Contextual Clues

Look for contextual clues. If the question includes a word you are not familiar with, look at the immediate context for some indication of what the word might mean. Contextual clues can often give you all the information you need to decipher the meaning of an unfamiliar word. Even if you can't determine the meaning, you may be able to narrow down the possibilities enough to make a solid guess at the answer to the question.

⊘ Prefixes

If you're having trouble with a word in the question or answer choices, try dissecting it. Take advantage of every clue that the word might include. Prefixes can be a huge help. Usually, they allow you to determine a basic meaning. *Pre-* means before, *post-* means after, *pro-* is positive, *de-* is negative. From prefixes, you can get an idea of the general meaning of the word and try to put it into context.

⊘ Hedge Words

Watch out for critical hedge words, such as *likely, may, can, often, almost, mostly, usually, generally, rarely*, and *sometimes*. Question writers insert these hedge phrases to cover every possibility. Often an answer choice will be wrong simply because it leaves no room for exception. Be on guard for answer choices that have definitive words such as *exactly* and *always*.

⊘ Switchback Words

Stay alert for *switchbacks*. These are the words and phrases frequently used to alert you to shifts in thought. The most common switchback words are *but, although*, and *however*. Others include *nevertheless, on the other hand, even though, while, in spite of, despite*, and *regardless of*. Switchback words are important to catch because they can change the direction of the question or an answer choice.

✓ FACE VALUE

When in doubt, use common sense. Accept the situation in the problem at face value. Don't read too much into it. These problems will not require you to make wild assumptions. If you have to go beyond creativity and warp time or space in order to have an answer choice fit the question, then you should move on and consider the other answer choices. These are normal problems rooted in reality. The applicable relationship or explanation may not be readily apparent, but it is there for you to figure out. Use your common sense to interpret anything that isn't clear.

Answer Choice Strategies

✓ ANSWER SELECTION

The most thorough way to pick an answer choice is to identify and eliminate wrong answers until only one is left, then confirm it is the correct answer. Sometimes an answer choice may immediately seem right, but be careful. The test writers will usually put more than one reasonable answer choice on each question, so take a second to read all of them and make sure that the other choices are not equally obvious. As long as you have time left, it is better to read every answer choice than to pick the first one that looks right without checking the others.

✓ ANSWER CHOICE FAMILIES

An answer choice family consists of two (in rare cases, three) answer choices that are very similar in construction and cannot all be true at the same time. If you see two answer choices that are direct opposites or parallels, one of them is usually the correct answer. For instance, if one answer choice says that quantity *x* increases and another either says that quantity *x* decreases (opposite) or says that quantity *y* increases (parallel), then those answer choices would fall into the same family. An answer choice that doesn't match the construction of the answer choice family is more likely to be incorrect. Most questions will not have answer choice families, but when they do appear, you should be prepared to recognize them.

✓ ELIMINATE ANSWERS

Eliminate answer choices as soon as you realize they are wrong, but make sure you consider all possibilities. If you are eliminating answer choices and realize that the last one you are left with is also wrong, don't panic. Start over and consider each choice again. There may be something you missed the first time that you will realize on the second pass.

✓ AVOID FACT TRAPS

Don't be distracted by an answer choice that is factually true but doesn't answer the question. You are looking for the choice that answers the question. Stay focused on what the question is asking for so you don't accidentally pick an answer that is true but incorrect. Always go back to the question and make sure the answer choice you've selected actually answers the question and is not merely a true statement.

✓ EXTREME STATEMENTS

In general, you should avoid answers that put forth extreme actions as standard practice or proclaim controversial ideas as established fact. An answer choice that states the "process should be used in certain situations, if..." is much more likely to be correct than one that states the "process should be discontinued completely." The first is a calm rational statement and doesn't even make a definitive, uncompromising stance, using a hedge word *if* to provide wiggle room, whereas the second choice is far more extreme.

✓ Benchmark

As you read through the answer choices and you come across one that seems to answer the question well, mentally select that answer choice. This is not your final answer, but it's the one that will help you evaluate the other answer choices. The one that you selected is your benchmark or standard for judging each of the other answer choices. Every other answer choice must be compared to your benchmark. That choice is correct until proven otherwise by another answer choice beating it. If you find a better answer, then that one becomes your new benchmark. Once you've decided that no other choice answers the question as well as your benchmark, you have your final answer.

✓ Predict the Answer

Before you even start looking at the answer choices, it is often best to try to predict the answer. When you come up with the answer on your own, it is easier to avoid distractions and traps because you will know exactly what to look for. The right answer choice is unlikely to be word-for-word what you came up with, but it should be a close match. Even if you are confident that you have the right answer, you should still take the time to read each option before moving on.

General Strategies

✓ Tough Questions

If you are stumped on a problem or it appears too hard or too difficult, don't waste time. Move on! Remember though, if you can quickly check for obviously incorrect answer choices, your chances of guessing correctly are greatly improved. Before you completely give up, at least try to knock out a couple of possible answers. Eliminate what you can and then guess at the remaining answer choices before moving on.

✓ Check Your Work

Since you will probably not know every term listed and the answer to every question, it is important that you get credit for the ones that you do know. Don't miss any questions through careless mistakes. If at all possible, try to take a second to look back over your answer selection and make sure you've selected the correct answer choice and haven't made a costly careless mistake (such as marking an answer choice that you didn't mean to mark). This quick double check should more than pay for itself in caught mistakes for the time it costs.

✓ Pace Yourself

It's easy to be overwhelmed when you're looking at a page full of questions; your mind is confused and full of random thoughts, and the clock is ticking down faster than you would like. Calm down and maintain the pace that you have set for yourself. Especially as you get down to the last few minutes of the test, don't let the small numbers on the clock make you panic. As long as you are on track by monitoring your pace, you are guaranteed to have time for each question.

✓ Don't Rush

It is very easy to make errors when you are in a hurry. Maintaining a fast pace in answering questions is pointless if it makes you miss questions that you would have gotten right otherwise. Test writers like to include distracting information and wrong answers that seem right. Taking a little extra time to avoid careless mistakes can make all the difference in your test score. Find a pace that allows you to be confident in the answers that you select.

⊘ Keep Moving

Panicking will not help you pass the test, so do your best to stay calm and keep moving. Taking deep breaths and going through the answer elimination steps you practiced can help to break through a stress barrier and keep your pace.

Final Notes

The combination of a solid foundation of content knowledge and the confidence that comes from practicing your plan for applying that knowledge is the key to maximizing your performance on test day. As your foundation of content knowledge is built up and strengthened, you'll find that the strategies included in this chapter become more and more effective in helping you quickly sift through the distractions and traps of the test to isolate the correct answer.

Now that you're preparing to move forward into the test content chapters of this book, be sure to keep your goal in mind. As you read, think about how you will be able to apply this information on the test. If you've already seen sample questions for the test and you have an idea of the question format and style, try to come up with questions of your own that you can answer based on what you're reading. This will give you valuable practice applying your knowledge in the same ways you can expect to on test day.

Good luck and good studying!

Reading

Literature

Explicit Information

Explicit information includes facts and statements that are found directly in a passage or a story. It is not information that is hinted at or information you need to make a conclusion about. Explicit information may be found in many forms; it can be contained in a quote as well as in a description. It can be found in dialogue and in actions. This information can sometimes be used to support an inference. The answers to questions about explicit information are found through careful reading of the text. Attention is given to pertinent facts or other information. In fiction, details about characters, events, and setting can be both explicit and implicit.

Read the following excerpt and identify the information that is explicit.

> According to an ancient Greek legend, an inventor named Daedalus was imprisoned on an island by an angry king. His son, Icarus, was with him. The inventor came up with an escape plan. He created two pairs of wings from feathers and a wooden frame. He made one for himself and one for his son.

Explicit information is information found directly in the text. It is not inferred; it is not suggested. The explicit information in this excerpt is about the Greek myth that tells the story of the inventor Daedalus. The excerpt says that the inventor Daedalus and his son Icarus were imprisoned on an island by an angry king. It says that he had a plan of escape, and that he created two pairs of wings from feathers and a wooden frame. This information is found directly in the excerpt. It is not necessary to make any inferences or guesses to obtain this information.

Inference

An inference is a conclusion that a reader can make based on the facts and other information in a passage or a story. An inference is based both on what is found in a passage or a story and what is known from personal experience. For instance, a story may say that a character is frightened and that he can hear the sounds of wolves in the distance. Based on both what is in the text and personal knowledge, it might be a logical conclusion that the character is frightened because he hears the sound of wolves. A good inference is supported by the information in a passage. Inferences are different from explicit information, which is clearly stated in a passage. Inferences are not stated in a passage. A reader must put the information together to come up with a logical conclusion.

Read the excerpt and decide why Jana finally relaxed.

> Jana loved her job, but the work was very demanding. She had trouble relaxing. She called a friend, but she still thought about work. She ordered a pizza, but eating it did not help. Then her kitten jumped on her lap and began to purr. Jana leaned back and began to hum a little tune. She felt better.

You can draw the conclusion that Jana relaxes because her kitten jumped on her lap. The kitten purred, and Jana leaned back and hummed a tune. Then, she felt better. The excerpt does not explicitly say that this is the reason why she was able to relax. The text leaves the matter unclear. But, the reader can infer or make a "best guess" that this is the reason she is relaxing. This is a logical conclusion based on the information in the passage. It is the best conclusion a reader can make based on the information he or she has read. Inferences are based on the information in a passage, but they are not directly stated in the passage.

Determining the Theme of a Passage

The theme of a passage is what the reader learns from the text or the passage. It is the lesson or moral contained in the passage. A passage can have two or more themes that convey its overall idea. The theme or themes of a passage are often based on universal themes. They can frequently be expressed using well-known sayings about life, society, or human nature, such as "Hard work pays off" or "Good triumphs over evil." Themes are not usually stated explicitly. The reader must figure them out by carefully reading the passage. Themes are often the reason why passages are written; they give a passage unity and meaning. Themes are created through plot development. The events of a story help shape the themes of a passage.

Explain why "Take care of what you care about" accurately describes the theme of the following excerpt.

> Luca collected baseball cards. But, Luca wasn't very careful with them. He left them around the house. His dog liked to chew. Luca and his friend Bart were looking at his collection. Then, they went outside. When Luca got home, he saw his dog chewing on his cards. They were ruined.

This excerpt tells the story of a boy who is careless with his baseball cards and leaves them lying around. His dog ends up chewing them and ruining them. The lesson is that if you care about something, you need to take care of it. This is the point of the story. The theme is the lesson that a story teaches. Some stories have more than one theme, but this is not really true of this excerpt. The reader needs to figure out the theme based on what happens in the story. Sometimes, as in the case of fables, the theme is stated directly in the text. However, this is not usually the case.

Components of a Story Summary

A summary of a passage or a story should include the main ideas of a passage and also the important details that support the main ideas. It shouldn't just be a general statement about what a passage is about, but should include important events and other details that make the story what it is. In order to write an objective summary, you have to reflect on what the passage is about. A summary puts the information in a concise form. Consequently, summarizing is different from paraphrasing. Paraphrasing involves rewording the main idea and supporting ideas in a fairly detailed way; summarizing does not. Summaries afford the reader the opportunity to quickly review the main points of a passage and the important details.

Setting and Characters

Without characters and setting, there is no story. They affect the plot of a story in many ways. The setting creates the background for the action. The setting could be someplace exotic or mundane, but wherever it is, it creates limitations for the characters. Characters are also essential to a story. They bring the story to life; it is their decisions, what they do, and how they act that creates the plot of a story and ultimately its theme. Characters can have good traits and bad traits. Analyzing what these are based on what a character does and says is an important aspect of comprehending the meaning of a story.

Read the excerpt and explain how the setting influences the plot.

> The cave was dark, so dark that Ernesto could not see a thing. He could not see his hand in front of him. He was lost, and he knew that time was running out. He could hear the trickle of water somewhere in the distance. He knew he had to follow the sound. It was his only hope of escaping.

The setting of the cave creates a conflict since Ernesto cannot see a thing and is lost. The excerpt also says that Ernesto's time is running out. While the reader does not know why this is the case, this increases the tension in the story. The fact that Ernesto can hear the dripping of the water is also important to the plot, since it influences the events of the story. Ernesto decides he should go towards the sound of the water. Setting influences the plot here because it creates a struggle for the main character. It also influences the character since Ernesto makes choices about what he should do based on the setting.

Impact of the Order of a Story or Introduction of Characters Has on a Story

The way in which an author chooses to order the events of or introduce characters in a story has a strong effect on it. Most stories are told in chronological order; one event occurs after another. But, an author can influence the development of a story by placing one event out of order to emphasize its importance. Another technique used by some authors is a flashback, in which time changes from the present to the past. When it comes to introducing characters, authors have a great deal of latitude. Authors often introduce the most important characters first so that the reader will have time to get acquainted with the characters' past and present situations. Readers are often influenced by the author's feelings toward a particular character, which often have an effect on how a character is introduced.

Determining the Meaning of Words or Phrases as They Are Used in a Text

When the reader does not understand a word or a phrase that is used in a passage or a story, it is important to examine the context clues around the word or phrase that provide hints about its meaning. Many words have more than one meaning, and it is only through an examination of the context that the reader can figure out the correct meaning. The word "crown" is a good example. This word has several meanings, including a coronet, the top of a head, the act of awarding something to someone, or even the act of hitting someone. Therefore, it is important to understand the context. In the sentence, "He sought to be crowned the winner of the competition," it is clear that the meaning is "to be awarded." Context must also be used to determine the meaning of phrases. In the sentence, "He wasn't going to stand for that anymore, so he told his boss off," the reader can use context to get a sense of the meaning of "going to stand for." In this case, the phrase means "not put up with."

Figurative Use of a Word

Authors use literary devices like figurative language to expand reality in a vivid way. An author can utilize figurative language to connect things in an exaggerated way, which results in a stronger, more vivid image. Examples of figurative language include simile, metaphor, personification, and hyperbole. Similes compare things using the comparing words *like* or *as*. "She is as brave as a lion" is an example of a simile. Metaphors compare things without using comparing words. An example of a metaphor is "She is a lion in the wild." Personification attributes human traits to an animal or non living thing. "Time flew by" is an example of personification. Hyperbole is an exaggeration that is not believable. "He waited in line for years" is an example of this literary device.

Read the excerpt; identify the form of figurative language represented by the phrase "like a fresh April shower," and explain your answer.

> We had been sequestered inside the barn all afternoon. It was hot, really hot. When the sun finally set and I opened the door, the evening air swept over us like a fresh April shower, leaving us ready to enjoy the evening.

The phrase "like a fresh April shower" is an example of a simile. The phrase compares the air with a fresh April shower and uses the word "like," so it qualifies as a simile. Similes compare two things using the word "like" or "as." This phrase is not a metaphor. Although it compares two things, it uses the word "like"; metaphors do not use either "like" or "as" to compare two things. It is not an example of personification, because nothing is being given human traits. There is no sign of hyperbole here either; there is no sense of an exaggeration.

Relationship Between the Denotative and Connotative Meaning of Words

The denotative meaning of a word and the connotative meaning are only alike in that, according to the dictionary, they mean the same thing. However, that is where the similarities end. The connotative meaning of a word is what is suggested above and beyond the literal meaning. For instance, the word "untidy" might mean "messy" or "unclean," whereas the word "slovenly" suggests something closer to "filthy." When writers create stories, they frequently use words that have strong connotations to describe and develop the characters and the setting. It is important for the reader to analyze these word choices to gain a better understanding of the author's purpose.

Read the following sentence.

I expected my gear to be inspected, but I never thought it would be scrutinized to this degree.

Explain the connotative meanings of the word "scrutinized" and how they relate to the word "inspected."

Both "scrutinized" and "inspected" have the dictionary meaning of being "closely looked at" or "studied." But, the word "scrutinized" means that something is being dissected and analyzed, not just inspected or checked out. The word "scrutinized" is a much stronger term than the word "inspected." Many things are inspected, but not everything is scrutinized. It is important to choose words that fit the situation, something that is done in this sentence. The connotations that a word brings to a sentence will impact the way a reader comprehends what is being written about. Words with strong connotations help a reader get a feel for what is being written about.

Impact of Words on Tone

Words can have a large impact on the tone of a passage. Tone is a result of the choice of language. For instance, when talking about or suggesting the mood of a person or a setting, it is vital to choose the right language to describe it. Is a person ecstatic, or is the person simply content? Is a room barren, or is it just empty? Similarly, using strong action verbs can create a tone that is forceful and remembered easily. The verb *buttress*, for instance, has a much stronger impact than the verb *strengthen*. Even though both words have basically the same meaning, the first one creates a more vivid image in the mind of the reader. It is important to use words that will be understood by the audience and will have the desired effect.

Fresh and Engaging Language

One way to get a reader's attention and hold it is to use language that is fresh and engaging. Using a personal point of view is a good way to accomplish this. You should try to generate excitement by using a different perspective. Always avoid clichés—they will come across as stale and worn out. Learning editing skills is useful; it will help you eliminate unnecessary portions of a text. Use a dictionary and a thesaurus to locate the words you are looking for, and analyze the words to determine how a reader might perceive them. Finally, read your passage aloud to see how it sounds.

Read the excerpt. Describe why the language is fresh and engaging.

"Full many a glorious morning have I seen

Flatter the mountain tops with sovereign eye,

Kissing with golden face the meadows green,

Gilding pale streams with heavenly alchemy;"

(Shakespeare, Sonnet XXXIII)

In these few lines, Shakespeare provides the reader with a fresh, new image of nature. Morning is personified as a romantic king in love with the meadows and streams. It is not just any morning, but *a glorious morning*, and it makes the mountain tops look even better than usual. Alchemy was a combination of magic and science thought to enable the creation of precious gold from ordinary metals, and the excerpt describes the streams as gilded, or covered with gold. The king himself is *kissing with golden face.* The lines are simple, and at the same time, sweet and poetic. The sun is the ruler of all. The writing is fresh and engaging.

Comedic or Tragic Resolution

When an author decides to include a comedic or tragic resolution in a story, the author is using a time-tested literary form that has existed for hundreds, even thousands, of years. The tragedy has a strict format. There is a tragic hero or protagonist who has a fatal flaw and becomes victim to it in the end. The play or story always ends sadly, with the hero in most cases dying or coming to some terrible end. A comedic resolution, on the other hand, always includes a happy ending. There are playful aspects to the plot and the ways in which the characters interact. These literary forms tell the reader what to expect in the story and how to assess the plot. They act as signposts as a reader proceeds through a text.

Understatement or a Sense of Irony

Many authors enjoy using a sense of irony or understatement as they write a story. Both techniques distance the writer from the characters and the events of a story. In either case, the reader must read between the lines to figure out what the author is actually getting at and what his or her point of view actually is. Understatement can be used as a humorous vehicle, allowing the author to comment on what is happening without being deeply emotionally invested in it. Irony allows the author to make a statement about what is really occurring without openly stating it. When reading a text, be sure to look for any underlying meaning that an author might be trying to convey. An initial reading of a text may not be enough to discern its true intended meaning. The way an author talks about what is happening often conveys that author's viewpoint of the events.

Satire vs. Sarcasm

Satire exposes the follies, foibles, and traditions of society, and is often humorous. A satire critiques the pretensions of powerful people in society. While criticism is intended, it is not overt, but rather implied. Mark Twain often employed satire to make a comment about the society in which his characters lived. Sarcasm is a type of humor that is meant to be insulting. Satire may employ the literary technique of irony, which is the tension between what is expected and what actually happens. Sarcasm is a sharp, bitter comment or remark that may or may not utilize understatement. It is an obvious criticism, and does not have the sophistication or creativity of satire, which is usually associated with an entire work. Sarcasm is usually limited to a comment.

Distinguishing between an Author's Point of View and What They May Say Literarily about a Character or a Situation

An author may use a wide array of literary techniques to discuss a topic, a character, or a situation, which could disguise the author's real feelings regarding what he or she is writing about. For instance, a writer might say that an area received a "little rain," when in fact the land might be flooded with water. Or, an author could describe a dent as "a little scratch" when there is actually an enormous dent. A reader must be able to put a writer's words into perspective to determine what has actually occurred.

The same is true when a writer uses irony to make a comment. Consider the following sentence: "I have little doubt that you will receive the praise that you deserve for your hard work." Taken at face value, this would be a compliment. However, if the situation is such that the recipient of the comment has made a complete fool of himself, the comment becomes irony, because the opposite of what is being said is true. Here again, the reader has to be careful to examine a situation described by a writer before jumping to conclusions about the author's viewpoint.

Ways in which Shakespeare's *Romeo and Juliet* is a timeless story

The story of a young man and woman falling in love and coming to a tragic end has been told over and over, and it represents a universal theme in literature. It was originally told by the Roman writer Ovid in his play *Pyramus and Thisbe*, which is a story of forbidden love. In modern times, a musical with a plot similar to *Romeo and Juliet* is *West Side Story*, which was in fact based on Shakespeare's play. It's important to note, however, that the theme was explored even before Shakespeare wrote his tragedy. Universal themes are found throughout literature. Even the Disney movie *Lady and the Tramp* has elements of the story of ill-fated love that is recounted in *Romeo and Juliet.*

> In what way is *Antigone* by the Greek writer Sophocles related to Henry David Thoreau's essay "Civil Disobedience"? In *Antigone*, the title character defies Creon, the ruler of Thebes, by invoking divine justice and breaking Creon's law to bury her brother. In his essay, Thoreau argues that people have a right and responsibility to rebel against laws that are immoral.

They are related because they share a universal theme of rebelliousness against laws that are unjust. Much of literature contains universal themes that repeat situations and ideals that humans live by. The fact that Antigone went against Creon shows that she had moral courage; the same is true of Thoreau, who argued against laws that were unjust. Even though *Antigone* is a play and was written long ago, it still relates to Thoreau's essay, which was written in the 19th century. Universal themes are timeless and are often repeated, but the context in which they are presented is affected by the times in which they are written.

Both Henry David Thoreau and Nathaniel Hawthorne were American writers of the 19th century. Thoreau's essays focused on the quiet desperation of man. Hawthorne's novels focused on characters who were struggling with the Puritanical background of America. Discuss the ways in which their viewpoints were different.

Thoreau was part of the Transcendental Movement that was awakening during the 19th century. It held that nature was a vital part of the human experience. Unlike the Puritanical viewpoint that people had little control over their destiny, the Transcendentalists believed that humans could choose their destiny. Thoreau was writing from this viewpoint, while Hawthorne was more concerned with the Puritanical legacy, which allowed little room for change or imagination. His books were a comment on this strict background, while Thoreau's essays were an exploration of a new world. Even though they wrote during the same century, their works represented different understandings of man's position in the universe.

Upton Sinclair's novel The Jungle is about an immigrant family's experiences working in a factory; John Steinbeck's novel The Grapes of Wrath is about a family of migrant workers suffering in the Dust Bowl of Middle America. They were both written in the early 20th century. Discuss why these authors most likely decided to write about these subjects.

These authors wrote about poor people in difficult situations; they were both concerned about social problems. This is a common theme of early 20th century literature, when the concept of helping the poor worker was just being introduced. One writer spoke of an immigrant family. The other based his novel on a migrant family. They would have had a lot in common, since both families were without roots. This theme is typical of the literature of the early 20th century, when so many immigrants were pouring into the United States. It was also timely because there were few laws restricting the kind of work that migrants could do

Importance of Being Able to Read and Comprehend a Wide Variety of Texts by the End of Grade 11 and Grade 12

It is important for an 11th grader to be able to read and comprehend literature—including stories, dramas, and poetry—in order to be well-versed in literature and how it reflects the various periods in which it was written. The student will develop a good background in the cultural aspects of writing, and will know how to respond to cultural references found in texts. The ability to read and comprehend literature will also help the student prepare for his or her future academic and career path.

The reasons why it is important for a student to be able to comprehend a wide variety of texts by the end of the 12th grade are manifold. This background will give the student a great advantage in terms of achieving success in school and the business world. Being widely read ensures greater knowledge of the world, helps a student become well-versed in cultural differences, and also gives the student a chance to develop his or her vocabulary and ability to express her or himself. Ultimately, having read a large number of different literary books will educate the student in many fields, and will help her or him become confident in our ever-complicated world, where communication is vital.

Informational Texts

Inference

An inference is a conclusion you can make based on the evidence in a passage. For instance, if a passage says that there are many people who ride bicycles to work, and that many people prefer riding a bike to driving a car, you might make the conclusion that riding a bike is fun. This is based on the information that you have on hand; it could be wrong, but it is the best guess you can make. Inferences need to have evidence that they are the most likely outcome. In this case, the fact that many people prefer riding a bike to work over driving a car leads the reader to conclude that riding a bike is fun.

Identify the Information in the Following Excerpt That Supports the Inference That Aluminum Is a Good Material for a Boat.

> Cement is heavy, and it can support weight. But, it sinks in water. Aluminum is light, and it does not rust easily. It floats easily. Bricks are made up of clay that is fired. They are fire resistant, and they last a long time. But, bricks are heavy.

The information that supports the inference that aluminum is a good material for a boat is that it is light and does not rust easily. Another supporting detail is that it floats easily. This is what the excerpt says. And this is the kind of evidence that is needed to support the inference identified in the question. The other details describe other materials, but they do not give information that suggests these materials would be good for a boat. Inferences are the best conclusions that can be made based on the information at hand.

DETERMINING THE CENTRAL IDEAS OF A PASSAGE

Central ideas are what a passage is mainly about. They are why the passage is written. The main idea is often found in a topic sentence or even a concluding sentence, and there are supporting details found in the passage that expand upon the main idea. There can, however, be more than one central idea, and these main ideas can be related and intertwined. For instance, the main or central idea of a passage may be that rainforests are drying out. A related main idea might be that the result of rainforest destruction is a loss of wildlife. These two central ideas are obviously related, and the passage may present both of them by focusing on one in one part of the passage and the other in another part of the passage. Another way they could be related is in a cause and effect relationship, with the loss of rainforests being the reason for losses of wildlife. It is important to always check to see if there is more than one central idea in a passage.

READ THE EXCERPT BELOW. IDENTIFY AND DISCUSS THE MAIN IDEA.

> Students who have jobs while attending high school tend not to have as much time to complete their homework as other students. They also do not have time for other activities. We should try to persuade our young people to concentrate on doing well in school, not to concentrate on making money. Having a job while you are a student is harmful.

The main idea of the excerpt is actually the last sentence: "Having a job while you are a student is harmful." This is what the excerpt is mostly about. The other sentences contain supporting information: students who have jobs don't have as much time for homework; students with jobs don't have time for as many activities. These are both supporting details that tell more about the main idea. The third sentence deals with a persuasive argument; it is another kind of detail. Only the last sentence tells what the excerpt is mostly about. Main ideas are sometimes found in a topic sentence at the start of a text or in the concluding sentence, which is the case in this excerpt.

SUMMARY OF AN INFORMATIONAL TEXT

A summary of an informational text should include the main idea or ideas of the passage and also the pertinent supporting details. A summary should not be a vague statement about what a passage is about, but should include important facts, events, or evidence that make the text a complete work. In order to write an objective summary, you need to think about what the text is saying, and then create a precise outline of the main idea and the important supporting information. Summarizing is not the same as paraphrasing. Paraphrasing involves rewording the main idea and supporting ideas in a fairly detailed way; summarizing does not. Summaries afford the reader the opportunity to quickly review the main points of a passage and the important details.

ANALYZING A TEXT

When you read a text, you need to pay attention. You need to watch for the introduction of ideas. You need to figure out how the ideas that are introduced are developed. When you read a complex text, it may be difficult to follow. Sometimes, it is hard to understand how one idea is linked to another idea. Sometimes, it helps to make an outline of a text. This will help you identify the main ideas. Then, you can figure out which ideas are supporting details. A complex text may also have vocabulary that you cannot understand. If you cannot figure out the meaning of certain words from the context, you can make a list of these words. Then, look them up in a dictionary. This will help you understand the meaning of the text.

Even an informational text tells a story. It introduces information, ideas, individuals, or events, and then provides details about them. A careful reader must learn to figure out the relationships between the details that an author includes and the ideas that the author introduced earlier in the text. Some of the information that is added may be used to supplement the description of an individual, an event, or an idea. Other information may be used to criticize an event, an idea, or an individual. It is up to the reader to have a discerning eye and decide what direction an author is taking by analyzing the author's language and viewpoint, as well as other information.

MEANING OF WORDS AND PHRASES

The meaning of words and phrases can typically be determined from the context of the sentence in which they appear, as well as the surrounding sentences. It may be necessary to read an entire text to figure out the meaning of a term, particularly a technical or legal term. While words may be used in a literal manner, phrases can be more difficult to figure out since their meaning is often not tied to the exact meaning of the words that comprise them. Phrases are often expressions that need to be interpreted. Expressions are idioms that are usually part of the vernacular of a language. They may require more effort to understand, although the meaning can often still be gleaned from the context.

DISCUSS THE MEANING OF THE PHRASE "JUMP SHIP" IN THE FOLLOWING SENTENCE.

> The start-up company wasn't working out the way that Hal and his partner hoped, and they thought it was time to jump ship and get into another business.

To figure out the meaning of the phrase "jump ship," the reader needs to look for context clues in the same way he or she would to figure out the meaning of a single word. The sentence says that the start-up company wasn't working out. It says that Hal and his partner thought it was time to get into another business. You can tell from the context of the sentence that the expression "jump ship" means to get out of something or to quit something. It has nautical overtones, and it comes from a nautical saying, but the context of the sentence makes it clear what the expression, or idiom, means. Although it might seem to have negative connotations, it does not necessarily have to be negative. It is a kind of final act, which could be construed as negative. However, the context of the sentence suggests that "jumping ship" in this instance might result in something positive occurring.

READ THE EXCERPT BELOW. USE THE CONTEXT CLUES TO DECIDE WHAT THE WORD "WATERLOO" MEANS IN THIS INSTANCE.

> Connie was worried that the competition was her Waterloo. She realized she wasn't Napoleon and she wasn't losing her entire kingdom because she lost a battle, but that's how it felt to her.

Using context clues is a good way to figure out the meanings of words and expressions without having to look them up in a dictionary. The way to discover context clues is to study the text. The excerpt says that Connie was worried that the competition was her Waterloo. This is obviously a reference to something, but it takes further analysis to figure out what it means. The next sentence talks about Napoleon and how he lost a kingdom because of a battle. One can draw the conclusion that "Waterloo" was probably the battle, and that someone's Waterloo is something that a person loses or does badly in. This helps the reader figure out the meaning of the word.

FIGURATIVE LANGUAGE

Figurative language is language that is used in a non-literal way. It allows the writer to expand the ways in which he or she uses language, making it more colorful and fresh. Figurative language takes a word or an expression that has a literal meaning and gives it a new one. For instance, an author might say that Lilli is like a graceful swan. While everyone knows that Lilli is a person, the image of Lilli as a graceful swan casts a new descriptive meaning. Figurative language takes many forms; it can be in the form of a simile, a metaphor, personification, or hyperbole. Similes compare things using the comparing words "*like*" or "*as.*" An example is, "Lilli is like a graceful swan." Metaphors compare things without using comparing words. An example is, "Lilli is a swan when she moves."

Personification attributes human traits to an animal or an inanimate object. An example is, "The swan spoke to Lilli."

READ THE EXCERPT FROM FORMER PRESIDENT GEORGE W. BUSH'S SECOND INAUGURAL ADDRESS.

> "...By our efforts, we have lit a fire as well - a fire in the minds of men. It warms those who feel its power, it burns those who fight its progress, and one day this untamed fire of freedom will reach the darkest corners of our world."

DISCUSS THE METAPHOR THAT FORMER PRESIDENT BUSH USES IN THIS EXCERPT.

The metaphor that President Bush uses is that of a fire of freedom that will grow in the minds of men and will warm those who feel its power. This fire is powerful, according to the metaphor, since it would burn those who fight against freedom. It is also powerful because it will reach all over the world. Bush uses the metaphor of a fire since it suggests light, and democracy is a kind of light that allows people to see the truth. That is why the metaphor is a powerful one. This is an example of how strong a metaphor can be in terms of getting a person's viewpoint and thoughts across to the public.

AGGRESSIVE VS. ASSERTIVE CONNOTATIONS

The words "aggressive" and "assertive" both describe someone with a strong nature. However, the word "aggressive" suggests someone who may be hostile or belligerent, while the term "assertive" could be interpreted to mean self-confident or self-assured. "Aggressive" has negative connotations when used to describe someone's nature, while the word "assertive" has more positive connotations. These words are examples of differences in connotations, since they both have meanings that go beyond what appears in the dictionary. Words like these should be chosen carefully, since they can convey a message about someone that may or may not be intended. When choosing words, a writer needs to look for the most accurate word to describe a person or a thing.

AUTHOR'S POINT OF VIEW

When an author writes a text, he or she must choose the structure that will work best for the text. For informational passages, there are several different structures an author can use. These include question and answer order, chronological or sequential order, problem and solution order, cause and effect order, and spatial order. Some texts use a combination of two or more of these structures depending on the breakdown of the topic. For persuasive documents, a question and answer order is often a good choice because it allows for a dramatic presentation of materials. This structure allows the author to highlight arguments for or against a position. A cause and effect order structure might also be a good choice for a persuasive text, and would also allow for the highlighting of arguments, as would a problem and solution order. Compare and contrast and order of importance are reasonable choices for informational pieces, and possibly for persuasive texts as well. Chronological ordering would be more suitable for an informational piece on a person or an event, where the points that are being made are not meant to convince the reader of something. The author should choose the structure that will best meet his or her writing goals.

VERONICA IS DOING A REPORT ON WHY PEOPLE SHOULD STOP THE KILLING OF WHALES. SHE IS TRYING TO FIGURE OUT WHICH TEXT STRUCTURE WOULD BEST HELP HER MEET HER GOAL TO OUTLINE THE REASONS WHY THIS HARVESTING WILL RESULT IN THE LOSS OF SPECIES THAT ARE IMPORTANT TO THE ENVIRONMENT. DESCRIBE WHICH TYPE OF ORDER WOULD PROBABLY WORK BEST FOR THIS REPORT, AND EXPLAIN WHY.

The best possible choices for the report would probably be either a problem and solution or a cause and effect organization, since they would allow the author to lay out the problem and the consequences of the killing of whales. A cause and effect order would show the immediate relationship between the killing of whales and its consequence; a problem and solution order would probably be best if the author wants to concentrate on the ways in which this practice is causing society problems and how the practice could be resolved. A compare and contrast structure would probably not work in this type of report. Finally, a chronological structure, which might be useful in part of the report to outline the past history of the practice, would probably not be a suitable structure for the entire report.

An author's point of view may be clear, or it may be hidden. It is important to read a text closely to find out exactly what the author thinks about the event, person, topic, or issue he or she is writing about. When reading, look for clues to the author's viewpoint in the form of emotional statements or critiques of others discussing the topic. Some authors make their viewpoints known only through rhetorical statements. These need to be analyzed closely to see if they should be taken at face value or if the author is somehow using rhetoric to exaggerate a point or to try to persuade the reader of something. Rhetoric can be a very effective vehicle that can draw a reader in through the use of elegant language. This is precisely why it is important to analyze an author's rhetoric to determine why he or she is employing it and what his or her goal might be. It is also vital to read the entire text before making any assumptions about an author's viewpoint.

THE PURPOSE OF THE RHETORIC IN THE FOLLOWING EXCERPT FROM A SPEECH BY FORMER PRESIDENT GEORGE W. BUSH.

> "Our opportunities are too great, our lives too short, to waste this moment. So tonight we vow to our nation. We will seize this moment of American promise. We will use these good times for great goals."

The President's purpose is clear; he wants to set an important goal for the public. In doing so, he is attempting to paint a picture of the importance of what he is saying. Phrases such as "Our opportunities are too great," "We will seize the moment," and "good times for great goals" set the stage for putting forth the President's agenda, which he hopes to present in the best possible light. Words have the capacity to transfix listeners with their elegance, a fact clearly illustrated by this excerpt. That is why speeches are so important to the political arena, and it is why excellent speech writers are extremely important to political candidates.

USING INFORMATION TECHNOLOGY SKILLS WISELY

Good information technology skills are necessary in order to sift through the enormous amount of information available on just about any topic. Before beginning any research, ask yourself how much information you think you are going to need; think about your target audience and their needs. Utilize search engines to make the task go faster. When evaluating multiple sources of information, do not rely solely on how recent they are. Consider the validity of sources as well. Do not rely on just one source. Using digital media is important because it allows you to broaden your scope beyond just words to include graphics and charts. Take the time to understand what online sources of information are available, which ones are most appropriate, and how they support one another.

USING THE REASONING THAT THE FOUNDING FATHERS BELIEVED THAT AFRICAN AMERICANS COULD NOT BE VIEWED AS CITIZENS AS DEFINED IN THE US CONSTITUTION, AND THEREFORE HAD NO RIGHTS BEFORE THE COURT, CHIEF JUSTICE TANEY'S MAJORITY OPINION IGNITED A FIRESTORM OF CONTROVERSY IN THE ALREADY HEATED DEBATE BETWEEN PRO- AND ANTI-SLAVERY ADVOCATES IN THE UNITED STATES DURING THE MID-19TH CENTURY. MANY OPPONENTS DECRIED THE CHIEF JUSTICE'S RULING AS ONE THAT WAS MOTIVATED BY POLITICS. ONE RESULT WAS THAT THE US CONGRESS COULD NO LONGER REGULATE SLAVERY ANYWHERE. THE DRED SCOTT DECISION IS VIEWED AS ONE OF A SERIES OF EVENTS THAT EVENTUALLY PUSHED THE COUNTRY INTO THE CIVIL WAR.

ANALYZE THE FOLLOWING EXCERPT FROM LINCOLN'S SECOND INAUGURAL ADDRESS IN 1865.

> "It may seem strange that any men should dare to ask a just God's assistance in wringing their bread from the sweat of other men's faces, but let us judge not, that we be not judged. The prayers of both could not be answered. That of neither has been answered fully..."

In this excerpt and in the address, Lincoln is talking about slavery. Like the majority of people of his time, Lincoln learned to read by studying the Bible. He makes frequent references to the Bible, and he often uses the rhetoric of the Bible to drive his point home. This is common in 19th century literary documents. When he says, "Wringing their bread from the sweat of other men's faces," he is paraphrasing from the Book of Genesis, which refers to physical work. Here, the word *bread* is used to refer to the wealth of the slave owners. Lincoln finds it strange that these slave owners should pray to the same God as those who do not own slaves for assistance in making money. He encourages his audience not to be hypocritical when he says, "let us judge not." This is a reference to the Book of Matthew of the Bible.

IMPORTANCE OF BEING A PROFICIENT READER OF LITERARY NONFICTION TEXTS BY GRADE 11 AND GRADE 12

It is extremely important for a student to be proficient in reading literary nonfiction texts by the end of grade 11. These types of texts will play a key role in the student's future life (and success). In other words, the ability to comprehend language and vocabulary will help the student attain the academic level he or she hopes to or the type of employment desired. In all walks of life, people need to be able to read and comprehend a variety of materials. This is why the ability to understand literary nonfiction texts is a valuable tool. It is especially important for those who hope to do well on college entrance examinations as well as other kinds of job examinations.

It is of the utmost importance for a 12th-grade student to be able to read literary nonfiction proficiently. Not only is it important for future academic endeavors (e.g., college and graduate school), but it is also vital to future career success. Whether it is reading a newspaper, an employee manual, or a science text, it is crucial that a person be comfortable when reading and be able to comprehend the material without extreme effort. Without this ability, a person will face limitations in his or her academia and business life. Communication is extremely important in today's workplace, and the foundation of this skill is being able to comprehend reading materials.

UNIVERSAL THEMES FOUND IN LITERATURE ARE AFFECTED BY THE TIME IN WHICH THE LITERATURE WAS WRITTEN

While universal themes are the same in terms of their meaning and what they depict or teach, the ways in which they are presented are affected by the time in which a literary piece was written. The characters and situations that are portrayed will mirror the environment in which the writer lived. Ancient literature depicts a time when myth was very much alive, and when the concept of personal freedom was still evolving and not taken for granted.

EVALUATE THE PURPOSE OF THE FOLLOWING EXCERPT FROM GEORGE WASHINGTON'S FAREWELL ADDRESS, WHICH WAS GIVEN ON SEPTEMBER 19, 1796.

> "The unity of government which constitutes you one people is also now dear to you. It is justly so, for it is a main pillar in the edifice of your real independence, the support of your tranquility at home, your peace abroad; of your safety; of your prosperity; of that very liberty which you so highly prize..."

This address given by the first president of the US when he announced that he did not want to run for re-election went over the groundwork that had established the new country. The passage stresses *the unity of government which constitutes you one people.* Washington truly believed that the US would be able to survive any attack, from without as well as from within, if it stayed with this principle. There is a hint that Washington foresaw the difficulties of holding together *the main pillar* (the different states) that were to come. His farewell address would go on to influence politicians and leaders for many years to come.

Writing

Clear and Coherent Writing

Clear and coherent writing requires good initial planning. You need to determine what you are going to say, who you are saying it to, and how you want to say it, as well as the kind of tone you want to project. In the process of writing, organize your arguments and use a logical order to develop them. Use paragraph breaks to help organize your thoughts. Your sentences should be precise and to the point. Make sure your punctuation is correct. Your ideas should be supported by evidence, and opposing ideas should be mentioned as well. When you get to your conclusion, avoid being repetitious; concentrate on summarizing. Proofread what you have written to check for any errors; reading the text aloud is often helpful.

Importance of Planning, Revising, Editing, and Reviewing a Text

Draw up a brief plan before you start to write so that you know what points you are going to cover. Once you have finished the writing, it is a good idea to set it aside for a time. That way, when you look at it again to see if revisions are needed, you will be approaching it with a fresh mind. During the process of editing, make sure you check for any grammatical, spelling, punctuation, or usage errors. Are your supporting details clear and presented in a logical order? Will your audience respond to your text? During your review process, you may feel that some sections need to be rewritten. Think about whatever criticism your peers or adults may have had about previous work as you review your writing.

Read the following passage, explain why it needs revision, and discuss how to revise it.

> Raising a puppy is more difficult. We all know how cute they are. Like kittens, they need a lot of care. So, don't be shocked that I tell you kittens are more cute.

The writer of these sentences has not made it clear what he or she is really trying to say. There is no organization, and there are grammatical and usage errors. A good revision would look like this:

> We all know how cute puppies and kittens are. They both require a lot of care, but I think puppies are more difficult to raise than kittens. I also think that kittens are cuter than puppies.

Here the thoughts are put down in a logical order. The writer makes a statement of fact (*puppies and kittens are cute*), and one of opinion (*I think...*), so it is clear what her preferences are. The passage now makes sense, and the writing is free from errors.

Conducting a Research Project

When conducting a short or a sustained research project to answer a question or solve a problem, it is a good idea to draw up a plan first. Then, make a list of keywords related to the question or problem. You can utilize these words either in a search engine or an online or print encyclopedia. Back issues of magazines, journals, and newspapers can also be used as source material. If you are synthesizing multiple sources, combine the similarities or the differences you have come up with. It is important that none of the information you gather be dated or untimely. All sources have to be cited following Modern Language Association (MLA) guidelines. Questions raised by your research should be explicit.

Using the Internet

Online sources that allow writers to get works published at little to no cost either as an e-book or a printed book are now widely available. There are editing as well as marketing services offered on many Internet sites. Writing tools offer help with everything from style to grammar. Sites for research are reliable, and offer accurate and objective information. Make sure you cite Internet sources using an accepted format such as that from the MLA (Modern Language Association). There are free online tools that can be accessed to allow people to work together on projects no matter how far apart they are geographically. Chat rooms and topic websites allow for an unprecedented exchange of information. Shared writing projects let you get adult input or brainstorm with your peers.

Gathering Relevant Information from Multiple Print and Digital Sources

Before compiling information from multiple print and digital sources, you must first decide how much information you need based on the scope of the project, and you must determine how knowledgeable your audience is. Make an outline of the similarities as well as the differences you encounter in various sources. Journals, text books, magazines, newspapers, and even texts written by other students: the number of sources you can uncover is limited only by your imagination. Strike a balance between being too detailed and bogged down, and too general and oversimplified. Whatever the source, verify how timely, accurate, and credible it is. You can avoid plagiarism, or using another person's words without acknowledgement, by following MLA (Modern Language Association) guidelines when you cite their works.

F. *Scott Fitzgerald's novel The Great Gatsby takes place on Long Island (near New York City) in the 1920s, during an era known as the Jazz Age. Discuss what the author's subject reveals about American society at that time.*

Fitzgerald was writing about a time when there was a period of great wealth in the country, as well as great excess and abandon, after the end of World War I. He portrays society's fascination with the ideals of wealth and happiness, the so-called "American Dream." The two main characters, Nick and Gatsby, both of whom served their country during the war, are cynical and disillusioned. Gatsby throws lavish parties at his estate every weekend with liquor (outlawed by the Eighteenth Amendment) flowing freely. Fitzgerald captures the mood with striking clarity, portraying the moral emptiness of the time and the growing distrust of the wealthy as the decade careened towards its close with the Great Depression of 1929.

Evaluate the purpose of the following excerpt from Franklin D. Roosevelt's speech of July 2, 1932.

"I pledge you, I pledge myself, to a new deal for the American people. Let us all here assembled constitute ourselves prophets of a new order of competence and of courage. This is more than a political campaign; it is a call to arms..."

In this speech given by Franklin D. Roosevelt when he accepted the Democratic nomination for President, he proposed launching a new effort to turn back the tide of Depression that had gripped the country for several years. In using the phrase "a call to arms," he addressed the audience in a manner similar to how a commander would address his soldiers. His purpose was to contrast himself and the Democratic Party with the Republican view of government, which favored big businesses and a continuation of the policies of Herbert Hoover. He subsequently went on to win in a landslide victory in November, and his policies, of course, went on to be labeled by history as The New Deal.

Make Writing a Habit

In today's information driven society, writing is a skill that is of utmost importance in adult life. Writing, whether it is a short paragraph or two or an extended thesis, should come easily and smoothly (and should even be second nature) for those who wish to be successful. As such, writing should become a habit. An adult who follows the old adage "the more you write, the better you write" is sure to achieve recognition in any field of endeavor. It is important to study the writing process—the conscious effort of note taking, writing drafts, editing, and revising—so that you will grasp the concept of fine tuning your writing to different audiences, and will feel equally at ease writing a short note or a thoroughly researched treatise.

Persuasive Text

Introducing an Argument in a Persuasive Passage

The best way to introduce an argument in a persuasive passage and to structure it is to begin by organizing your thoughts and researching the evidence carefully. You should write everything down in outline format to start. Make sure you put the claim at the beginning of the passage. Then, list the reasons and the evidence that you have to support the claim. It is important that you provide enough evidence. Reasons and evidence should follow each other in a logical order. Write the passage so that you hold the reader's attention; use a strong tone and choose words carefully for maximum effect. If you can get the reader to understand your claim, he or she will be more likely to agree with your argument. Restate your claim in the concluding paragraph to maximize the impact on the reader.

Making a Claim

When making a claim, it is important to first think about the arguments that support that claim. While researching, try to anticipate what readers might say; this will help you thoroughly develop your claim. It is not enough to research a claim on the Internet, because many sources are dubious at best. Look for sites that are objective. Find authorities that you can quote, and use statistics. Present counterclaims using ample evidence. Mention both the strengths and weaknesses without any prejudice. Divide each counterclaim into a separate paragraph with supporting evidence. Make sure to present everything in a logical manner so that the information will be easily understood by the reader. Most importantly, one needs to separate opinions from facts.

Creating Cohesion

The best way to create cohesion between claims and evidence is to organize your ideas, and then write sentences explaining your reasons and evidence that logically follow your main ideas. Careful research will result in your argument being cohesive and easy to understand. Your claim and evidence must be clearly related to each other. Sometimes, it is useful to include metaphors, similes, or analogies to make your point clearer. Words and phrases that will indicate to the reader that the claim and evidence are related include "since," "because," "as a consequence," and "as a result." You can also utilize clauses to demonstrate a relationship between the reason and the effect. This approach is illustrated in the following sentence: "Since the sun now rose earlier in the morning, the birds awakened earlier and began their song." The first clause sets the tone, and it establishes causality between the reason and the effect. After writing, reread your text to verify that the relationships between cause and effect are logical.

Formal Style

A formal style is important when you want your writing to be objective and precise. A few requirements must be met to achieve this. It is important not to use fragments; write in complete sentences. Avoid contractions, and do not change tenses between sentences or paragraphs. Do not use the words "I" or "you"; this will add a more serious tone to your writing. Whenever possible, avoid using the passive tense. Using the active voice will make your writing more focused and interesting. Ensure your spelling is correct and that you follow all punctuation rules. Finally, make sure your ideas are presented in a logical order.

READ THE FOLLOWING PASSAGE AND SUGGEST SOME WAYS TO MAKE IT MORE FORMAL.

> When I was a kid growing up, I remember I had a lot of hard times. As a teenager, other kids used to make fun of me and call me names. It was really depressing. I couldn't find anyone to take to the prom. Sometimes, it was hard to keep up with all my homework.

HERE IS ONE WAY TO REWRITE IT:

> Becoming a teenager can be a stressful time. Adolescence involves both physical and emotional changes. Peer pressure and pressure at school cause many teenagers to have anxiety disorders; some even suffer from mild to severe depression. Boys and girls both worry about their physical appearance and about being popular.

The account is presented in the third person to make the passage more authoritative and formal. Complex sentences are utilized to keep the writing varied and interesting. Personal emotions are expressed in a more objective manner. A higher level of vocabulary results in a more precise, informed, and impressive finished text.

CONCLUDING STATEMENT

A concluding statement is an important part of a persuasive passage because it sets the tone for the reader and adds a sense of completion. A concluding sentence should not just repeat what was already said; the concluding statement should tie everything together. The concluding sentence should basically restate the importance of the argument. By doing this in the concluding paragraph, the impact on the reader will be maximized, and you will be more likely to bring the reader over to your side of an argument. The conclusion should logically fit into the flow of your passage. A good concluding statement serves to cement the bonds you have developed with the reader, and provides one more opportunity to get the reader on your side.

WHAT KIND OF ARGUMENT WOULD THE FOLLOWING CONCLUDING SENTENCE BE BEST SUITED FOR?

> As a result, soccer is the most popular sport in the world.

The sentence makes a good concluding sentence for a passage about the reasons why soccer (called football outside of the US) is the most popular sport in the world. Arguments can include the fact that players do not need any special equipment, while players of a similar sport—American football—need equipment such as helmets and protective padding. Another good angle is the fact that players don't have to be a certain size to play soccer, whereas the sport of American football places a premium on very large players, especially when filling defensive positions. Basketball, another sport that is also popular, requires a wooden court and two metal baskets with nets installed at a certain height. The concluding sentence provided would tie all the elements of the argument together.

Informational or Explanatory Text

INTRODUCING A TOPIC

An informational or explanatory text should have an introduction to the topic that the text will cover. One way you can accomplish this is by using a topic sentence, with details that support your thesis included afterwards. Another tactic is to use a reference to something going on in the modern world, even if your topic relates to something in the past. This makes your topic immediately more relevant. Some writers like to preview the ideas and concepts they are going to discuss by showing their relevance to a main topic. You could also preview concepts by demonstrating how they relate to everyday life.

Developing a Topic

It is important to develop the topic of an informational or explanatory text by utilizing relevant facts that clearly support the main topic. Include a topic sentence followed by any supporting details. These details should preferably be concrete facts that you have carefully researched, and which you are certain are accurate. You can also provide quotes taken from known experts in a field that is relevant to your topic. Quotes not only lend credibility to your thesis, but can also make your writing more varied and interesting. Diverse multimedia techniques, charts, and examples will also enhance your presentation. However, you should make sure these techniques play a supportive role, and are not presented solely to make your text look flashy.

Creating Cohesion

Experienced writers know how to use appropriate transitions to create cohesion in a text. They serve to clarify the relationships between ideas and concepts. Transition words or phrases such as "consequently," "therefore," and "as a result of" indicate causality between ideas. "However," "on the other hand," "in contrast," "but," and "similarly" indicate a compare and contrast relationship. You can also draw attention to examples by using words and phrases like "namely," "for example," "for instance," and "that is." When you need to show the order of importance of ideas or concepts, use transitions such as "at first," "primarily," "secondly," "former," or "latter."

Using Precise Language and Domain-Specific Vocabulary

Writers of informational or explanatory texts must use precise language and domain specific vocabulary in order to accurately get their ideas across. General vocabulary words will not bring home the points you are trying to make. Your audience will not follow your thesis closely if the text lacks the details that are supplied by carefully chosen, precise, and domain specific language. Using the word "isobar" in a text about meteorology, for instance, would be more effective than using the word "pressure." During the research stage, make sure you closely study the vocabulary used. Use a dictionary to clarify the meanings of words and terms you do not understand.

Establishing and Maintaining a Formal Style

Experienced writers use a formal style when they are writing explanatory or informational texts to lend greater credence to their material. They do not use an informal or colloquial tone, and they utilize the third person for objectivity. They use complex sentences, which are longer and add a further tone of formality and depth to the subject. By using a formal style, they show that they are serious about their subject. They are striving to make supporting details clear and to the point, but they are also presenting them in as much complexity as the intended audience can absorb. There is no introduction of personal opinion, unless that opinion can be carefully justified.

Importance of a Good Concluding Statement

A good concluding statement should sum up the overall intention of the text, and serves to "wrap up" the passage so that the reader is aware that you arrived at the logical ending of your argument. The conclusion should review the most salient points that you made, the reasoning you employed, and the supporting arguments for your reasoning. It serves to reinforce in the reader's mind that you did not leave anything out. The reader should not feel that there is more pertinent information that may follow. A good conclusion allows the reader to sit back and weigh the overall impact of your thesis, and it greatly increases the effectiveness of a text.

Narratives

Setting the Stage

To set the stage for a narrative, you need to introduce the reader to the setting and the characters. Next, you should introduce a plot line. This should consist of various events that lead to a problem, a climax, and a resolution. This gives a narrative structure. The way in which the author introduces these elements has an influence on the overall effectiveness of the narrative. Make sure to use language to describe the setting and the characters that will grab the reader's attention. Make the details specific. The conclusion or resolution will allow you to tie up the details of the story.

Introducing a Narrator

The narrator in a story is the person doing the "speaking," or the one who is telling the story. A narrator can speak in the first or third person. The narrator can shift from one person to another during the course of the story. It is even possible for the narrator to be non-human. The introduction of your narrator can be quick, subtle, dramatic, or humorous; it is up to you. Many times, an event or a circumstance opens the story. Make sure any details about time, place, and circumstance are developed logically and naturally, and that the reader will understand who (or what) the narrator is and where the narrator fits into the story.

Using Techniques

Writers employ numerous techniques to bring a narrative to life. Dialogue is one tool; it gives the reader a sense of what is happening, and also adds color and nuance to characters or the narrator. What a character says and how he says it portrays how that character feels. Pacing is also used in a narrative. The rhythms of the sentences, whether they are short or long, allow a writer to use time to the best effect, and to add color and depth to the events in the narrative. The plot line or sequence of events in the narrative is the actual structure of the story, and is developed from the opening of the story through one or more actions. These actions eventually lead to a climax, and then a resolution. The use of descriptions lets the reader visualize what is happening.

Interjecting Sequence

Sequence should come in an order that can be easily grasped by the reader. It is a function of a natural flow of events, dialogue, and plot. Sequence should enhance what is happening in the story, and it should never seem forced or unnatural. A pattern should emerge, and it must make sense to the reader. Often times, a writer will make use of a flashback, a literary device where the writer goes back in time, and where events do not follow in sequence. When crafted properly, the flashback will make sense in the context of the story. Flashbacks can often add a sense of mystery or suspense to a narrative. Chronological narration, which puts events in the order in which they happened, is another literary device, and is used more frequently than flashbacks.

Using Precise Language

Precise language is important in a narrative. It helps ensure that the concepts you are trying to communicate are readily understood by the audience. Precise language will be livelier, and will provoke more thought on the part of the reader. It includes the proper use of dialogue and imagery to get the point of the story across as succinctly as possible, so that there is nothing vague in the narrative. Your use of language should show an articulate grasp and control of the plot, and the whole text should be cohesive. Sensory language (which brings up images of the senses) can add extra detail and feeling, and can be very persuasive. Understanding the full range of language will result in a better narrative.

IMPORTANCE OF THE CONCLUSION

The conclusion to a narrative is extremely important. An inadequate or poorly thought out conclusion can leave the reader confused and unable to tie everything together, or "wrap things up." There must be some type of resolution to whatever was described in the opening and the events that followed. A conclusion is not repetition; it is resolution. The resolution can be a summary. It could be a quotation. The resolution does not have to be clear cut. In fact, it may leave a lot unanswered. It could end with a rhetorical question or questions. Indeed, unlike traditional writing, conclusions in modern literature often present more questions than answers. In every case, however, the conclusion will leave the reader with no doubt that the narrative is over.

DOREEN IS WRITING A SHORT STORY ABOUT TRAINING HER DOG LOLA TO COMPETE IN AN AGILITY COMPETITION. SHE HAS WRITTEN ABOUT ALL THAT SHE HAS DONE TO TRAIN HER DOG OVER THE PAST THREE MONTHS. SHE IS PREPARING TO WRITE A CONCLUSION TO HER STORY. DESCRIBE WHAT DOREEN SHOULD TRY TO ACCOMPLISH WITH HER CONCLUSION.

Doreen should write a conclusion to tie everything together. Since she was training her dog Lola to compete, the end of the story should tell whether Lola won the competition. Doreen should describe the day of the competition and the result. This is the most obvious conclusion for her story. Doreen should bring her story to a close with a fitting and appropriate ending so that the reader will know exactly what the outcome was, and will not be left hanging in the end. The opening and all the events that happened lead up to this, and there is a form to her story.

Speaking and Listening

Discussions

Preparing for a Discussion on a Particular Topic

It is exceedingly important to prepare for class discussions. These discussions are important because they help prepare students for future discussions, and also allow them to practice effective techniques and learn communication skills. The exchanging of ideas is a skill that will remain with a student throughout his or her lifetime. When preparing for such a discussion, a student should research the subject at hand using the Internet and other sources. They should make sure they have read all essential applicable information. It is also important to have the resources (quotes, statistics, and audio visual material) you will need during the discussion on hand. A useful technique is to rehearse your role; practice the day before with a family member or a friend. Determine what you are going to focus on. If you are leading the discussion, think ahead about how you are going to guide the discussion to a conclusion, and how much time will be needed.

Rules for Collegial Discussions

Properly organized collegial discussions can be very productive, and can result in many new and interesting ideas being formulated and brought out in the classroom. It is important that rules be set up to promote civil, democratic discussions. Guidelines for the discussion should be established, which should include how much time each participant will be allowed to talk and then respond. There should be clear roles. Specific goals need to be established, and the progress towards reaching those goals should be tracked, with a deadline for completion kept in mind. Participants should learn how to use questions to add detail and depth to the discussion, and how to build on and further ideas that are put forth by others. It is important to try to understand and communicate with individuals who have a different perspective, especially from a cultural point of view. Everyone should be able to make use of evidence, and should be able to express themselves clearly within the structured framework.

Ways to Pose Questions That Elicit Elaboration

Asking questions that will encourage a response from others and propel a conversation entails asking specific, not general, questions, since they force the listener to think. Ideally, questions should be open-ended (i.e. they can't be answered with a simple "yes" or "no"). It is important to be proficient at asking questions, and at learning the art of asking the right question. Being a good listener is key to asking good questions. You should build on the ideas expressed by others in the classroom. One technique is asking a question at the end of what you have to say. You could ask something like, "Does that answer your question?" This helps personalize questions. Another overlooked technique is to take notes. It is also important to prevent people from straying from the subject by taking control of the situation and diplomatically steering the conversation back to the subject at hand.

Ensuring That a Full Range of Positions Are Equally Covered

Guidelines for the discussion should stress allowing each member of the team to express his or her viewpoint without prejudice. Each member should receive the same amount of time to put forth a theory or thesis, or to address a subject through an analytical probe without interruption. On the other hand, every team member should also be granted time to respond to individual presentations. Emotional outbursts do not have a place in this kind of discussion, nor do personal comments that pull away from an objective and intelligent discussion. When there is a divergence of opinion, the greatest of respect should be given to the opposing viewpoints.

Respond to Diverse Perspectives

Key to responding to diverse perspectives is listening and keeping an open mind. Divergent ideas could be compiled by the entire discussion group in a list. Then, the link between the ideas could be identified, and it might be determined through consensus which opinions require more scrutiny or research. A goal should be set for the investigation or task, and assignments made so that any further research that is needed is done. The conversation can then resume with this new additional information kept in mind. This process is an orderly means of reaching a deeper understanding of a topic that not everyone may agree with or about.

Integrating Various Sources of Information That Are Presented in Diverse Formats and Media

There are many different sources of information. On the Internet, there are multiple sites (some more reliable than others) where print information as well as charts and other graphic organizers are available to all. In addition, there are hard copy and online journals, textbooks, magazines, and newspapers; researchers are often overwhelmed with information. It is best to choose only the sources that can be verified or are from a credible author or organization. This information must then be analyzed to see how consistent it is and whether valid discrepancies exist, and why. After, it can be used in a presentation or a discussion.

Analyzing a Speaker's Point of View

The point of view of a speaker needs to be determined to evaluate whether there is a clear delineation between evidence and the speaker's theory. If a speaker's viewpoint is prejudiced or based on emotion, this needs to be identified by evaluating the evidence. It is important to evaluate a speaker's choice of words and tone to determine whether the speech is tinged with feeling or objective. The evidence that a speaker uses to back up claims must also be closely evaluated to determine its source and validity. Many speakers are able to influence an audience through their strength of delivery, but if studied, there may be holes in logic or faults in the evidence that is used to prove a point.

Presenting Claims, Findings, and Supporting Evidence

When in a focused discussion, be prepared to present your claims, findings, and supporting evidence in a clear and distinct manner. This means being prepared. When compiling your data, make sure to create an outline that has the main ideas and then the supporting evidence, including graphics that you want to present. Attention to details will result in a successful presentation, one in which the diverse individuals in the group will come away with a feeling of having been part of something meaningful. Facts and examples should be stressed. Repetition creates retention. It is important for the speaker to choose the right words, and to build momentum by gradually building up to the strongest argument(s). Graphics are important, because participants will be more convinced if they can see evidence as well as hear it. By breaking up the flow of the discussion and introducing pauses before and after pertinent arguments, the speaker will make the presentation of facts more interesting.

Presentations

One way to bring a presentation to life is to use digital media, including graphics, audio, visual, and interactive elements. Such tools will not only make a presentation more interesting and memorable, but will also keep those listening from distancing themselves from the presentation. It is easy for audience members to become bored during a presentation if they don't feel included. Digital media can effectively hold their interest. Graphics, diagrams, charts, and maps all serve to reinforce the point you are trying to make. The simpler these forms of media are, the more effective they will be. They serve to help the audience understand your argument; a video or audio can enhance the claims and findings of a presentation. Both visuals and multimedia components should be considered aids; they are not going to do the work for you. It is useful to rehearse the presentation until it flows smoothly.

When giving a speech, you need to make sure you feel confident in front of your audience. Exchange nerves for a funny story to open; have a variety of multimedia graphics that will pull your audience in. Perhaps most important, use the English language correctly when you speak. This is a situation where using correct grammar is essential. Before you speak, write your speech out and make sure that it demonstrates a command of correct conventions. In addition, be sure to speak clearly and slowly, and to enunciate words. Make sure the words that you choose have the correct literal meaning and the intended connotations. Try to avoid hesitations that end with "uh" or "er," which only distract from what you are saying. Look at one person in the audience and talk to her or him. Maintaining a smile will help create an atmosphere of informality. Extra effort needs to be made to avoid being wordy. Redundancy is sure to make audience attention wander.

Eye contact is one of the most important tactics for an effective presentation. When you maintain eye contact with audience members, you can be assured that your listeners will find your presentation believable. They will also be more likely to remember what you said. Reading a speech instead of giving one will have little impact on your audience. Make sure to look people in the eyes and smile. Use a voice that can be easily heard, and enunciate words so people will not be left wondering what was said. Remember to adapt your voice to the task at hand. Are you trying to persuade, look for sympathy, or tell an amazing story? All of these scenarios should yield a different voice and way of presenting the material. Most important of all, relax!

Language

Usage is a Matter of Convention

Latin is an ancient language. It does not change. But English, like any modern language, may change over time. New words are always being introduced into the English language. Words are adapted from other languages. Examples of adapted words are taco, pizza, and karaoke. Usage, which is a matter of convention, can also change and evolve over time. It is not always clear what the correct form is, since there are sometimes two possibilities. For instance, the use of the subjunctive is much less prevalent today than it was in the past. The answer to the question of whether it is acceptable to begin a question with the word "and" or "but" has also changed. Years ago, this was strictly against usage rules, but it is now common practice in less formal texts.

Use of the Serial Comma

The rules regarding use of the serial comma differ depending on whether a text is academic or more informal. Traditionally, and in academia, a comma is always used before the "and" in a list of items. This is not the case in more casual texts, such as newspapers, where the convention is not to use a comma before the word "and" in a list of items. This is just one example of how usage conventions are not always rigid, and can change according to the usage of the moment. A general rule of thumb is that a comma should be used in front of the "and" in a list of items if the text is for a school-related or academic use, but should not be used if the text is intended for everyday use.

Marina and Keegan are writing a report together. They are having a disagreement about whether a split infinitive Marina used in one sentence is grammatically correct. Marina thinks the split infinitive is fine in this instance, but Keegan does not agree. How can they come to a resolution about this issue?

There are many grey areas related to English usage, and split infinitives is one of them. The strict notion that they should never be used is less in vogue today than it was a few years ago, and they may now even be found in formal writing. However, if the text that is being prepared is academic, it is probably best to avoid using them. In English, it is always possible to word things differently to avoid awkward usage, and this is also true for split infinitives. Marina and Keegan could consult *Merriam-Webster's Dictionary of English Usage* or *Garner's Modern American Usage* to figure out what they should do. Typically, however, the more academic the paper, the more formal the usage should be.

Rules of Hyphenation

Hyphens are used in many instances. They are used to join compound words, whether nouns or verbs. The best way to determine if a word needs a hyphen is to check it in the dictionary. They are used to separate two or more adjectives when they come before a noun. They are used to hyphenate all compound numbers from *twenty-one* through *ninety-nine*. They are used to hyphenate all spelled-out fractions. They are used to hyphenate prefixes when they come before proper nouns. They are used to hyphenate all words beginning with *self* except *selfish* and *selfless*. They are used in some titles, such as vice-president. It is important not to confuse a hyphen with a dash.

Correct the punctuation in the following sentence.

> The forty year old man jumped over the bramble covered fence rail, where he came upon a too good to be true treasure chest filled with gold pieces that were really chocolate candies.

THE CORRECT WAY TO WRITE THIS SENTENCE IS: THE FORTY-YEAR-OLD MAN JUMPED OVER THE BRAMBLE-COVERED FENCE RAIL, WHERE HE CAME UPON A TOO-GOOD-TO-BE-TRUE TREASURE CHEST FILLED WITH GOLD PIECES THAT WERE REALLY CHOCOLATE CANDIES.

Hyphens are used to join several adjectives modifying a noun when they cannot be joined by the word "and." "Forty," "year," and "old" all modify man and are hyphenated; these modifiers cannot be joined by "and." The same is true of "bramble covered." It would be awkward to say bramble and covered. The two words work together to create a description, so they are hyphenated. The last group of adjectives is "too," "good," and "to be true," which is really an expression that needs to be hyphenated. It is important not to confuse a hyphen with a dash; a dash is used to punctuate clauses, not adjectives. Although not shown here, hyphens are also used to punctuate titles such as "vice-president."

COMMON SPELLING ERRORS

CORRECT THE SPELLING IN THE SENTENCE BELOW.

> The visitors will aclimate to the envirommment as soon as they become accustomed to the surroundings of the tropacs.

The words that are misspelled are "aclimate," which should be "acclimate"; "environmment," which is spelled "environment"; and "tropacs," which is spelled "tropics." It is important to learn to spell words correctly. One way to learn how to spell words is to learn how to sound out words. Break longer words down into syllables, and into affixes and roots. Get the correct spelling from a dictionary, and then practice that spelling. Practice with a few words at a time; use them in sentences. Then move on to new vocabulary words. It is also useful to remember spelling rules, such as "i before e except after c" (receive), "drop the final e" (like, liking), and "double the last consonant" when adding suffixes (stop, stopped).

SYNTAX

Syntax is the order of the words in a sentence. When writing, it is important to make sure not only that the syntax is correct, but also that it is not repetitive. There is nothing worse than reading a passage that has sentences that are all alike: noun, verb, object. These need to be interspersed with sentences that use a variety of clause constructions. This will lend a musicality to the writing, and will allow for greater flow of language and ideas. Make sure to reread any written material to ensure that the syntax is correct and engaging. Otherwise, you may end up with something that comes off as confused rather than well-written.

REWRITE THE FOLLOWING SENTENCES BY VARYING THEIR SYNTAX.

> Marilyn and Rosemary worked together. They were having a party. They had to get all the food done first. They cleaned the house and decorated. They invited about 20 people. The people were all work associates. They were having the party in Marilyn's backyard. This is where she had many similar parties. They were always fun.

THIS IS ONE WAY TO REWRITE THE SENTENCES SO THAT THE SYNTAX IS VARIED:

Marilyn and Rosemary, who worked together, were going to have a party. But before they could do that, they had to get all the food ready for it, as well as clean the house and decorate. They invited about 20 people, who were all work associates, and were holding the party in Marilyn's backyard, where there had been many other parties that were always fun.

The rewritten sentences provide a greater variety of syntax, and consequently, greater rhythm. The language is more engaging as a result. Remember to make use of clauses to introduce information and create sentences that are complex. In addition, remember to reread any work you rewrite to make sure it makes sense.

Context Clues

The term "context clues" refers to the words or phrases in the sentences that surround a new word or phrase. Context clues can often allow the reader to figure out the meaning of an unfamiliar word or phrase. Context clues may include examples of the new word or phrase, synonyms, antonyms, definitions, or contrasting information. By using context clues in the surrounding sentences, the reader can figure out approximately what the unknown word or phrase means. The placement of a word or a phrase is important, as is its function in a sentence. If a word or a phrase is being used as an adjective, the reader should look at the other adjectives in the sentence or the surrounding sentences to see if there is a clue to the word's or phrase's meaning. The location of a word or a phrase is also important. For instance, if a word or a phrase is at the beginning of a sentence, try to figure out its consequence; this may help the reader figure out its meaning.

Using context clues, determine the meaning of "fortuitous" as it is used in the following excerpt.

> Warren felt that meeting his nephew was quite fortuitous, since his nephew showed a real interest in getting involved in the company's business. Warren was hopeful that someday his nephew could take over for him.

To figure out the meaning of the word "fortuitous," the reader needs to analyze the rest of the sentence, as well as the following sentence. It would appear that their meeting was a good thing, since Warren was hopeful that his nephew could take over for him. The adjective "hopeful" helps the reader come to the conclusion that "fortuitous" means good or lucky. This is just one of the context clues. Another one would be that the nephew showed a real interest in his uncle's business. Always make sure to study the surrounding phrases and sentences for clues to an unknown word. The placement of the word or phrase and its function in the sentence are also important.

Explain how context clues can help the reader figure out the meaning of the phrase "prosthetic device" in the following excerpt.

> Modern artificial limbs are much better than artificial limbs of the past. These prosthetic devices have made it possible for amputees to run and to compete in sports. For instance, Vietnam veteran Bill Demby is able to play basketball in an aggressive, fast-paced, competitive manner thanks to high-tech plastic legs.

The placement of the phrase "prosthetic devices" helps the reader understand that the phrase is another way of saying "modern artificial limbs." This is the subject of the excerpt; the term "prosthetic devices" is a synonym for "modern artificial limbs." Even if the reader does not understand the meaning of "prosthetic," he or she can figure out the meaning of the expression. This shows how placement and context clues can assist a reader in learning the meaning of a word or an expression. Always study the information in an excerpt to better understand what is being said. The conclusion of the second sentence reinforces the meaning of the phrase by providing another synonym: "high-tech plastic legs."

How Certain Endings Can Indicate What Part of Speech a Word Is

The suffix of a word can be extremely important in telling a reader what function the word has in a sentence. Certain endings are used to make a stem an adjective; others are used to make a stem a noun. For instance, the root *consider* has many forms. It becomes a noun—*consideration*—with the addition of *-ation*. It becomes an adjective—*considerate*—with the addition of the suffix *-ate*. The adverb *considerately* can be made from the adjective *considerate* by adding *-ly*. This is a simple yet sophisticated method of figuring out what part of speech a word is.

The root word for *absolution* is *absolute*. The suffix *-tion* indicates that the word is a noun. The root could be combined with other suffixes to make other parts of speech as well. Add an *-ly* and you have the adverb *absolutely*. This word is a noun in its root form (*absolute*), so no change is needed to it. To make the verb *absolve*, the suffix *-ve* is added. This word is irregular, since most roots tend to be in verb form. It is important to be able to analyze a word, not just for its etymology, but also to determine what part of speech the word might be.

Discuss the Etymology of the Word Fluctuate in the Following Sentence.

Tommy's mother noticed that his emotions tended to *fluctuate* a lot.

There really isn't a context clue in this statement, so you need to look up the word and discover its etymology to learn more about its meaning. The dictionary says that *fluctuate* is an intransitive verb, meaning it has no object. There are three syllables: fluc.tu.ate. The word has a Latin origin. It is derived from the verb "fluctuare," which means to undulate. You will also need to look up the word "undulate." It means to move in a wave-like motion, or to change continually. Synonyms of *fluctuate* are "alter," "shift," "swing," and "hesitate." In this usage, you can also see that there is a connotation of unpredictability. These clues give you a better understanding of the statement.

Using Specialized Reference Materials to Determine the Pronunciation of a Word

A print or digital dictionary can be used to find out many things about a word. A dictionary will show the correct pronunciation of a word, provide its meaning, and identify what part of speech the word is. It will also tell how the word was derived—that is, what words it came from originally. A dictionary will have a guide that shows how to sound out the words; it will use symbols to indicate sounds, and will also use sample sounds (the "a" in "bad," for instance). A dictionary lists all of the meanings of a word and the parts of speech the word can be used as. A thesaurus is useful because it lists synonyms for all the various meanings of a word, and it can help you clarify the precise meaning of a word as it is used in the text you are reading. This means you can find other words to use in a report or a text that mean the same thing as a word that may be used too often. Many books will have a glossary at the end to help you understand difficult or unfamiliar words used in the text.

Read the Sentence Below. Determine the Meaning of "A Partisan Response."

While at the meeting of the homeowners' association, Jeannie had the distinct feeling that there was a partisan response when all the other tenants belligerently shouted that they were just not going to accept any more increases in maintenance assessments, no matter what the condition of the roof was.

The meaning of the phrase can be determined from the context clues in the sentence. One big clue is the fact that the "other tenants belligerently shouted..." This suggests a tone of prejudice or unreasonableness. The sentence further suggests that there was something wrong with the roof that needed repairing, and that "no matter what," the other tenants were not willing to pay. Therefore, the reader can come to the conclusion that the phrase refers to a prejudiced reaction or response. If there were not enough clues in the sentence to determine the phrase's meaning, the word "partisan" could be looked up in a dictionary. Its meaning would explain the meaning of the phrase.

Analyze the Following Statement by Jesus Christ, Which Is Found in the New Testament of the Bible.

"If anyone comes to me and does not hate his own father and mother and wife and children and brothers and sisters, yes, and even his own life, he cannot be my disciple. And whoever does not carry their cross and follow me cannot be my disciple."(Luke 14:25-27)

This statement by Jesus that is quoted by Luke is an example of hyperbole. Hyperbole, or exaggeration to make a point, is frequently used throughout the Bible. It is not meant to be taken literally, and there is no command to hate family members or oneself. Rather, it is an entreaty that is meant to arouse intense emotion for maximum effect. The next sentence offers a clue in context for the reader's interpretation: one must be able to carry one's own cross (work hard) to be a disciple of Christ (i.e. to be a devout Christian). Therefore, the meaning is that devotion to God is more important than any relationship to any other family member, or any self-interest.

Nuances of "superfluous" and "outmoded"

Nuances are slight differences in the meanings of words that mean nearly the same thing. Nuances give words different tones or shades of meaning. They are similar to connotations, although usually more subtle. In the case of the words "superfluous" and "outmoded," superfluous conveys the sense that something is not and probably was never needed, while outmoded simply suggests that something is no longer of value since it is rendered needless due to age. Writers often use nuance to suggest something rather than saying it directly. This is often done through the choice of word or words that are used. Readers should always be aware of nuances, and should take them into account when considering the overall intent of a text.

Comprehension

It is important to acquire and accurately use words and phrases at the appropriate level to improve comprehension of various school subjects. Comprehension of academic and domain specific words is crucial to understanding the ideas and theories you will encounter as you move further in your academic career or enter the work force. Increased word knowledge that is domain specific helps individuals attain their academic and career goals. Therefore, it is very important to develop a system for increasing vocabulary through reading, using word lists, understanding word etymologies, and using new words in academic or work-related settings. A good vocabulary will result in greater personal achievements at a variety of levels.

Practice Test #1

Practice Questions

QUESTIONS 1-5 PERTAIN TO THE FOLLOWING EXCERPT.

Excerpt from Act 3, Scene 1 of Hamlet

by William Shakespeare

Enter HAMLET

HAMLET: To be, or not to be: that is the question:
Whether 'tis nobler in the mind to suffer
The slings and arrows of outrageous fortune,
Or to take arms against a sea of troubles,
And by opposing end them? To die: to sleep;
No more; and by a sleep to say we end
The heart-ache and the thousand natural shocks
That flesh is heir to, 'tis a consummation
Devoutly to be wish'd. To die, to sleep;
To sleep: perchance to dream: ay, there's the rub;
For in that sleep of death what dreams may come
When we have shuffled off this mortal coil,
Must give us pause: there's the respect
That makes calamity of so long life;
For who would bear the whips and scorns of time,
The oppressor's wrong, the proud man's contumely,
The pangs of despriz'd love, the law's delay,
The insolence of office and the spurns
That patient merit of the unworthy takes,
When he himself might his quietus make
With a bare bodkin? Who would fardels bear,
To grunt and sweat under a weary life,

But that the dread of something after death,
The undiscover'd country from whose bourn
No traveller returns, puzzles the will
And makes us rather bear those ills we have
Than fly to others that we know not of?
Thus conscience does make cowards of us all;
And thus the native hue of resolution
Is sicklied o'er with the pale cast of thought,
And enterprises of great pith and moment
With this regard their currents turn awry,
And lose the name of action. —Soft you now!
The fair Ophelia! Nymph, in thy orisons
Be all my sins remember'd.
OPHELIA: Good my lord,
How does your honour for this many a day?
HAMLET: I humbly thank you; well, well, well.
OPHELIA: My lord, I have remembrances of yours,
That I have longed long to re-deliver;
I pray you, now receive them.
HAMLET: No, not I;
I never gave you aught.
OPHELIA: My honour'd lord, you know right well you did;
And, with them, words of so sweet breath composed
As made the things more rich: their perfume lost,
Take these again; for to the noble mind
Rich gifts wax poor when givers prove unkind.
There, my lord.
HAMLET: Ha, ha! are you honest?

OPHELIA: My lord?

HAMLET: Are you fair?

OPHELIA: What means your lordship?

HAMLET: That if you be honest and fair, your honesty should admit no discourse to your beauty.

OPHELIA: Could beauty, my lord, have better commerce than with honesty?

HAMLET: Ay, truly; for the power of beauty will sooner transform honesty from what it is to a bawd than the force of honesty can translate beauty into his likeness: this was sometime a paradox, but now the time gives it proof. I did love you once.

OPHELIA: Indeed, my lord, you made me believe so.

HAMLET: You should not have believed me; for virtue cannot so inoculate our old stock but we shall relish of it: I loved you not.

OPHELIA: I was the more deceived.

HAMLET: Get thee to a nunnery: why wouldst thou be a breeder of sinners? I am myself indifferent honest; but yet I could accuse me of such things that it were better my mother had not borne me: I am very proud, revengeful, ambitious, with more offences at my beck than I have thoughts to put them in, imagination to give them shape, or time to act them in. What should such fellows as I do crawling between earth and heaven? We are arrant knaves, all; believe none of us. Go thy ways to a nunnery. Where's your father?

OPHELIA: At home, my lord.

HAMLET: Let the doors be shut upon him, that he may play the
fool no where but in's own house. Farewell.

OPHELIA: O, help him, you sweet heavens!

HAMLET: If thou dost marry, I'll give thee this plague for
thy dowry: be thou as chaste as ice, as pure as
snow, thou shalt not escape calumny. Get thee to a
nunnery, go: farewell. Or, if thou wilt needs
marry, marry a fool; for wise men know well enough
what monsters you make of them. To a nunnery, go,
and quickly too. Farewell.

OPHELIA: O heavenly powers, restore him!

HAMLET: I have heard of your paintings too, well enough; God
has given you one face, and you make yourselves
another: you jig, you amble, and you lisp, and
nick-name God's creatures, and make your wantonness
your ignorance. Go to, I'll no more on't; it hath
made me mad. I say, we will have no more marriages:
those that are married already, all but one, shall
live; the rest shall keep as they are. To a
nunnery, go.

Exit

1. In this excerpt, Hamlet wonders if it is better to deal with unlucky circumstances or avoid them completely by dying. Which lines from the excerpt provide evidence of Hamlet's consideration?

a. For in that sleep of death what dreams may come / When we have shuffled off this mortal coil,
b. Thus conscience does make cowards of us all; / And thus the native hue of resolution / Is sicklied o'er with the pale cast of thought, / And enterprises of great pith and moment
c. Ay, truly; for the power of beauty will sooner / transform honesty from what it is to a bawd than the / force of honesty can translate beauty into his / likeness
d. 'tis nobler in the mind to suffer /The slings and arrows of outrageous fortune, /Or to take arms against a sea of troubles, / And by opposing end them?

2. How does Shakespeare resolve Hamlet's questions about life and death in the monologue that opens this excerpt?

a. Hamlet says he will continue questioning life and death once Ophelia leaves.
b. Hamlet leans toward not killing himself because he is afraid of death.
c. Hamlet decides to explore the undiscovered country of death.
d. Hamlet is so angry that he cannot come to a conclusion about life and death.

3. Although Hamlet does not kill himself, some critics interpret his distancing of himself from loved ones such as Ophelia as a kind of self-imposed death. Is this a valid interpretation?

a. Yes, because interacting with loved ones is the only thing that makes life worth living.
b. No, because Hamlet seems to have little regard for his loved ones.
c. Yes, because a person no longer can interact with loved ones in death.
d. No, because his loved ones still can interact with him by force.

4. In what way is Hamlet's greeting to Ophelia ironic?

a. Hamlet tells her he is well even though he just had been contemplating his own death.
b. Hamlet tells her he is humble even though he clearly is quite conceited.
c. Hamlet tells Ophelia he has never given her gifts even though she insists he has.
d. Hamlet calls Ophelia a "pretty lady" even though he later contradicts this compliment.

5. Like Hamlet, the character "Willy Loman" in Arthur Miller's Death of a Salesman is undone by his trust in forces outside himself. Specifically, the changing economy ruins Willy, and Hamlet's power-hungry uncle ruins him. Willy ultimately kills himself. How does this action compare to Hamlet's treatment of his own problems in the excerpt?

a. Both Willy and Hamlet believe that bad situations always work themselves out in the end. Therefore, not becoming involved in such situations' outcomes is best.
b. Both Willy and Hamlet realize that the economy and power are changeable things. Therefore, one person cannot influence them.
c. Both Willy and Hamlet feel like victims and see death as a way of conquering the forces working against them, but only Willy goes through with it.
d. Both Willy and Hamlet commit themselves to death, thereby taking an active role in their personal fates.

QUESTIONS 6-10 PERTAIN TO THE FOLLOWING EXCERPT.

Excerpt from Emma

by Jane Austen

Emma Woodhouse, handsome, clever, and rich, with a comfortable home and happy disposition, seemed to unite some of the best blessings of existence; and had lived nearly twenty-one years in the world with very little to distress or <u>vex</u> her.

She was the youngest of the two daughters of a most affectionate, indulgent father; and had, in consequence of her sister's marriage, been mistress of his house from a very early period. Her mother had died too long ago for her to have more than an indistinct remembrance of her caresses; and her place had been supplied by an excellent woman as governess, who had fallen little short of a mother in affection.

Sixteen years had Miss Taylor been in Mr. Woodhouse's family, less as a governess than a friend, very fond of both daughters, but particularly of Emma. Between them it was more the intimacy of sisters. Even before Miss Taylor had ceased to hold the nominal office of governess, the mildness of her temper had hardly allowed her to impose any restraint; and the shadow of authority being now long passed away, they had been living together as friend and friend very mutually attached, and Emma doing just what she liked; highly esteeming Miss Taylor's judgment, but directed chiefly by her own.

The real evils, indeed, of Emma's situation were the power of having rather too much her own way, and a disposition to think a little too well of herself; these were the disadvantages which threatened her many enjoyments. The danger, however, was at present so unperceived, that they did not by any means rank as misfortunes with her.

Sorrow came—a gentle sorrow—but not at all in the shape of any disagreeable consciousness—Miss Taylor married. It was Miss Taylor's loss which first brought grief. It was on the wedding-day of this beloved friend that Emma first sat in mournful thought of any continuance. The wedding over, and the bride-people gone, her father and herself were left to dine together, with no prospect of a third to cheer a long evening. Her father composed himself to sleep after dinner, as usual, and she had then only to sit and think of what she had lost.

The event had every promise of happiness for her friend. Mr. Weston was a man of unexceptionable character, easy fortune, suitable age, and pleasant manners; and there was some satisfaction in considering with what self-denying, generous friendship she had always wished and promoted the match; but it was a black morning's work for her. The want of Miss Taylor would be felt every hour of every day. She recalled her past kindness—the kindness, the affection of sixteen years—how she had taught and how she had played with her from five years old—how she had devoted all her powers to attach and amuse her in health—and how nursed her through the various illnesses of childhood. A large debt of gratitude was owing here...the equal footing and perfect unreserve which had soon followed Isabella's marriage, on their being left to each other, was yet a dearer, tenderer recollection. She had been a friend and companion such as few possessed: intelligent, well-informed, useful, gentle, knowing all the ways of the family, interested in all its concerns, and peculiarly interested in herself, in every pleasure, every scheme of hers—one to whom she could speak every thought as it arose, and who had such an affection for her as could never find fault.

How was she to bear the change?—It was true that her friend was going only half a mile from them; but Emma was aware that great must be the difference between a Mrs. Weston, only half a mile from them, and a Miss Taylor in the house; and with all her advantages, natural and domestic, she was now in great danger of suffering from intellectual solitude. She dearly loved her father, but he was no companion for her. He could not meet her in conversation, rational or playful.

The evil of the actual disparity in their ages (and Mr. Woodhouse had not married early) was much increased by his constitution and habits; for having been a valetudinarian all his life, without activity of mind or body, he was a much older man in ways than in years; and though everywhere beloved for the friendliness of his heart and his amiable temper, his talents could not have recommended him at any time.

Her sister, though comparatively but little removed by matrimony, being settled in London, only sixteen miles off, was much beyond her daily reach; and many a long October and November evening must be struggled through at Hartfield, before Christmas brought the next visit from Isabella and her husband, and their little children, to fill the house, and give her pleasant society again.

6. How does Miss Taylor's marriage affect Emma?

a. Miss Taylor's marriage disrupts the comfort Emma had enjoyed all her life.
b. Emma is happy her friend is marrying a wonderful man.
c. Emma regards the change as a challenge and opportunity for intellectual growth.
d. Miss Taylor's marriage makes Emma think about getting married herself.

7. As used in the first paragraph, what does the word vex mean?

a. interest
b. fulfill
c. support
d. displease

8. Based on this excerpt, Emma can be described as

a. unfortunate.
b. devious.
c. selfish.
d. studious.

9. How do themes of class and maturity interact in this excerpt?

a. Emma's upper-class background gives her greater access to education, thereby making her more interested in intellectual stimulation than a less mature person might be.
b. The privilege that comes with an upper-class background can prevent a person from having the necessary skills for dealing with change in a mature way.
c. Emma's first twenty-one years were so happy because she enjoyed a privileged, upper-class lifestyle, and that happiness made her a more mature person.
d. Having people constantly take care of her has prevented Emma from developing feelings of kindness and love for others.

10. Why does the author describe Miss Taylor's wedding as a "black morning's work"?

a. Emma has to work to pretend she is happy about the wedding.
b. The day of Miss Taylor's wedding is a bad day for Emma.
c. Emma worked hard to organize the wedding.
d. The wedding party dresses in black.

QUESTIONS 11-15 PERTAIN TO THE FOLLOWING EXCERPT.

Excerpt from The Federalist No. 1

By Alexander Hamilton

To the People of the State of New York:

AFTER an unequivocal experience of the inefficacy of the subsisting federal government, you are called upon to deliberate on a new Constitution for the United States of America. The subject speaks its own importance; comprehending in its consequences nothing less than the existence of the UNION, the safety and welfare of the parts of which it is composed, the fate of an empire in many respects the most interesting in the world. It has been frequently remarked that it seems to have been reserved to the people of this country, by their conduct and example, to decide the important question, whether societies of men are really capable or not of establishing good government from reflection and choice, or whether they are forever destined to depend for their political constitutions on accident and force. If there be any truth in the remark, the crisis at which we are arrived may with propriety be regarded as the era in which that decision is to be made; and a wrong election of the part we shall act may, in this view, deserve to be considered as the general misfortune of mankind.

This idea will add the inducements of philanthropy to those of patriotism, to heighten the solicitude which all considerate and good men must feel for the event. Happy will it be if our choice should be directed by a judicious estimate of our true interests, unperplexed and unbiased by considerations not connected with the public good. But this is a thing more ardently to be wished than seriously to be expected. The plan offered to our deliberations affects too many particular interests, innovates upon too many local institutions, not to involve in its discussion a variety of objects foreign to its merits, and of views, passions and prejudices little favorable to the discovery of truth.

Among the most formidable of the obstacles which the new Constitution will have to encounter may readily be distinguished the obvious interest of a certain class of men in every State to resist all changes which may hazard a diminution of the power, emolument, and consequence of the offices they hold under the State establishments; and the perverted ambition of another class of men, who will either hope to aggrandize themselves by the confusions of their country, or will flatter themselves with fairer prospects of elevation from the subdivision of the empire into several partial confederacies than from its union under one government.

It is not, however, my design to dwell upon observations of this nature. I am well aware that it would be disingenuous to resolve indiscriminately the opposition of any set of men (merely because their situations might subject them to suspicion) into interested or ambitious views. Candor will oblige us to admit that even such men may be actuated by upright intentions; and it cannot be doubted that much of the opposition which has made its appearance, or may hereafter make its appearance, will spring from sources, blameless at least, if not respectable—the honest errors of minds led astray by preconceived jealousies and fears. So numerous indeed and so powerful are the causes which serve to give a false bias to the judgment, that we, upon many occasions, see wise and good men on the wrong as well as on the right side of questions of the first magnitude to society. This circumstance, if duly attended to, would furnish a lesson of moderation to those who are ever so much persuaded of their being in the right in any controversy. And a further reason for caution, in this respect, might be drawn from the reflection that we are not always sure that those who advocate the truth are influenced by purer principles than their antagonists. Ambition, avarice, personal animosity, party opposition, and many other motives not more laudable than these, are apt to operate as well upon those who support as those who oppose the right side of a question. Were there not even these inducements to moderation, nothing could be more ill-judged than that intolerant spirit which has, at all times, characterized political parties. For in politics, as in religion, it is equally absurd to aim at making proselytes by fire and sword. Heresies in either can rarely be cured by persecution.

And yet, however just these sentiments will be allowed to be, we have already sufficient indications that it will happen in this as in all former cases of great national discussion. A torrent of angry and malignant passions will be let loose. To judge from the conduct of the opposite parties, we shall be led to conclude that they will mutually hope to evince the justness of their opinions, and to increase the number of their converts by the loudness of their declamations and the bitterness of their invectives. An enlightened zeal for the energy and efficiency of government will be stigmatized as the offspring of a temper fond of despotic power and hostile to the principles of liberty. An over-scrupulous jealousy of danger to the rights of the people, which is more commonly the fault of the head than of the heart, will be represented as mere pretense and artifice, the stale bait for popularity at the expense of the public good. It will be forgotten, on the one hand, that jealousy is the usual concomitant of love, and that the noble enthusiasm of liberty is apt to be infected with a spirit of narrow and illiberal distrust. On the other hand, it will be equally forgotten that the vigor of government is essential to the security of liberty; that, in the contemplation of a sound and well-informed judgment, their interest can never be separated; and that a dangerous ambition more often lurks behind the specious mask of zeal for the rights of the people than under the forbidden appearance of zeal for the firmness and efficiency of government. History will teach us that the former has been found a much more certain road to the introduction of despotism than the latter, and that of those men who have overturned the liberties of republics, the greatest number have begun their career by paying an <u>obsequious</u> court to the people; commencing demagogues, and ending tyrants.

11. How does the opening of this excerpt affect the writer's argument?

a. By criticizing the United States Constitution explicitly, he is challenging readers to look at old institutions in new ways that may have positive effects on the federal government.
b. By portraying the subsisting federal government as suffering from inefficacy, he is seeking to alienate overly patriotic readers.
c. By saying that it is up to "the people of this country" to establish a "good government," he is suggesting that he expects input from his fellow Americans regarding how to improve the United States Constitution.
d. By drawing attention to the "unequivocal" "inefficacy" of the subsisting federal government, Alexander Hamilton immediately explains why the federal government is in need of change.

12. What effect does the author's use of first-person point of view have on his argument?

a. It attempts to establish agreement between the reader and himself.
b. It establishes an informal tone that makes him seem friendlier and more approachable.
c. It forces the reader to feel responsibility for the federal government's problems.
d. It implies the reader also needs to suggest methods for improving the federal government.

13. Which of the following sentences from the excerpt exemplifies an attempt to sway the reader's opinion of the writer's opponents?

a. And yet, however just these sentiments will be allowed to be, we have already sufficient indications that it will happen in this as in all former cases of great national discussion.
b. For in politics, as in religion, it is equally absurd to aim at making proselytes by fire and sword.
c. To judge from the conduct of the opposite parties, we shall be led to conclude that they will mutually hope to evince the justness of their opinions, and to increase the number of their converts by the loudness of their declamations and the bitterness of their invectives.
d. This idea will add the inducements of philanthropy to those of patriotism, to heighten the solicitude which all considerate and good men must feel for the event.

14. Why does the writer follow paragraph 3 by stating, "It is not, however, my design to dwell upon observations of this nature"?

a. He regrets criticizing politicians currently holding office and wants the reader to focus on the less inflammatory details in his argument.
b. He wants to give the impression that the purpose of his argument is not merely to criticize politicians who are currently holding office.
c. He realizes he lacks the information to continue criticizing politicians currently holding office and cannot continue his argument.
d. He believes that criticizing politicians currently holding office is a weak way to present his argument and will stop doing so.

15. As used in the final sentence of the excerpt, what does the word obsequious mean?

a. submissive
b. free
c. revolutionary
d. dominant

QUESTIONS 16-20 PERTAIN TO THE FOLLOWING EXCERPT.

Second Inaugural Address

By Abraham Lincoln

Fellow-Countrymen:

AT this second appearing to take the oath of the Presidential office there is less occasion for an extended address than there was at the first. Then a statement somewhat in detail of a course to be pursued seemed fitting and proper. Now, at the expiration of four years, during which public declarations have been constantly called forth on every point and phase of the great contest which still absorbs the attention and engrosses the energies of the nation, little that is new could be presented. The progress of our arms, upon which all else chiefly depends, is as well known to the public as to myself, and it is, I trust, reasonably satisfactory and encouraging to all. With high hope for the future, no prediction in regard to it is ventured.

On the occasion corresponding to this four years ago all thoughts were anxiously directed to an impending civil war. All dreaded it, all sought to avert it. While the inaugural address was being delivered from this place, devoted altogether to saving the Union without war, insurgent agents were in the city seeking to destroy it without war—seeking to dissolve the Union and divide effects by negotiation. Both parties deprecated war, but one of them would make war rather than let the nation survive, and the other would accept war rather than let it perish, and the war came.

One-eighth of the whole population were colored slaves, not distributed generally over the Union, but localized in the southern part of it. These slaves constituted a peculiar and powerful interest. All knew that this interest was somehow the cause of the war. To strengthen, perpetuate, and extend this interest was the object for which the insurgents would rend the Union even by war, while the Government claimed no right to do more than to restrict the territorial enlargement of it. Neither party expected for the war the magnitude or the duration which it has already attained. Neither anticipated that the cause of the conflict might cease with or even before the conflict itself should cease. Each looked for an easier triumph, and a result less fundamental and astounding. Both read the same Bible and pray to the same God, and each invokes His aid against the other. It may seem strange that any men should dare to ask a just God's assistance in wringing their bread from the sweat of other men's faces, but let us judge not, that we be not judged. The prayers of both could not be answered. That of neither has been answered fully. The Almighty has His own purposes. "Woe unto the world because of offenses; for it must needs be that offenses come, but woe to that man by whom the offense cometh." If we shall suppose that American slavery is one of those offenses which, in the providence of God, must needs come, but which, having continued through His appointed time, He now wills to remove, and that He gives to both North and South this terrible war as the woe due to those by whom the offense came, shall we discern therein any departure from those divine attributes which the believers in a living God always ascribe to Him? Fondly do we hope, fervently do we pray, that this mighty scourge of war may speedily pass away. Yet, if God wills that it continue until all the wealth piled by the bondsman's two hundred and fifty years of unrequited toil shall be sunk, and until every drop of blood drawn with the lash shall be paid by another drawn with the sword, as was said three thousand years ago, so still it must be said "the judgments of the Lord are true and righteous altogether."

With malice toward none, with charity for all, with firmness in the right as God gives us to see the right, let us strive on to finish the work we are in, to bind up the nation's wounds, to care for him who shall have borne the battle and for his widow and his orphan, to do all which may achieve and cherish a just and lasting peace among ourselves and with all nations.

16. Why does Lincoln discuss his first inaugural address in this passage?

a. To prove that the country could have gone in a different direction.
b. To illustrate how the country had changed since his first inauguration.
c. To show how much he improved the country during his first term.
d. To explain that the country was once a place of peace.

17. Which sentence from the address supports the idea that Lincoln believed the North and the South did not have equally justifiable reasons for taking part in the war?

a. All knew that this interest was somehow the cause of the war.
b. Neither anticipated that the cause of the conflict might cease with or even before the conflict, itself, should cease.
c. Both parties deprecated war, but one of them would make war rather than let the nation survive, and the other would accept war rather than let it perish, and the war came.
d. Each looked for an easier triumph, and a result less fundamental and astounding.

18. How does Lincoln unite the themes of war and religion in his second inaugural address?

a. He suggests that the war and its end are parts of God's plan.
b. He says that no man would ask God to help him win a war.
c. He insists that it is God's responsibility, not his own, to resolve the war.
d. He quotes from the Bible liberally in order to extend an address he knew was too short.

19. How might reading Lincoln's address online differ from hearing it in person?

a. Lincoln likely was angry while reading his address, and this anger is lost in its translation to online text.
b. Lincoln's original address was much longer than the version that later appeared online.
c. Lincoln was an impressive-looking man, and this characteristic could be conveyed online only if the web page includes a photograph of him.
d. Lincoln would have been able to use his voice to heighten the emotion in his address.

20. What is the purpose of the final paragraph of Lincoln's address?

a. It is a sober remembrance for all who died during the American Civil War.
b. It is a warning that America could face new conflicts with other nations.
c. It is an attempt to forge a new feeling of union and caring between the North and the South.
d. It is a plea to other nations to seek peaceful solutions to conflicts with the United States.

THE FOLLOWING QUESTIONS ARE NOT ABOUT A PASSAGE. READ AND ANSWER EACH QUESTION.

21. Which of the following would be the best source to begin developing a position about civil rights for an oral debate?

a. A blog created by a proponent of civil rights
b. An interview with someone who took part in a civil rights march
c. A history textbook detailing civil rights
d. A speech by a famous civil rights leader

22. Which of the following is essential in the concluding statement of an argument?

a. The introduction of new points that might lead to future arguments.
b. A summary of the issue that reinforces clearly its main points.
c. A contradiction of the argument's main points to provide fresh perspectives.
d. An unrelated detail that might lighten the audience's mood after a heated debate.

23. Read the sentences, and then answer the question that follows.

I often have heard arguments claiming that complete freedom of speech could lead to dangerous situations. Without complete freedom of speech, we are hardly living in a free society.

Which word would best link these sentences?

a. However
b. Therefore
c. So
d. Supposedly

24. Which of the following choices would be most essential to an argument in favor of global environmental protection?

a. a personal story about how you have witnessed the destruction of the environment in your own neighborhood
b. a newspaper editorial about illegal garbage dumping
c. a photograph of a rain forest damaged by pollution
d. scientifically supported statistics detailing how pollution has damaged the environment throughout the world

25. Which of the following statements would best conclude an essay about playwright William Shakespeare?

a. William Shakespeare died of unknown causes on April 23, 1616.
b. William Shakespeare wrote the most important plays ever written, and I think his best one is definitely *Romeo and Juliet.*
c. William Shakespeare's plays have been staged in theaters throughout the world, yet he will always be most closely associated with the Globe Theater in London.
d. Although William Shakespeare died in 1616, the artistry and eternal relevance of his work destined it to thrive for hundreds of years into the future.

26. Which of the following statements best would open an informative essay about filmmaker Alfred Hitchcock?

a. Probably the best filmmaker of all time is Alfred Hitchcock, whose best movies were The Birds and Vertigo.
b. In the history of cinema, few filmmakers had as far-reaching effect on the medium as Alfred Hitchcock.
c. Alfred Hitchcock's movies may be old, but they're still entertaining enough to entertain modern audiences.
d. Alfred Hitchcock was a really famous director who made some awesome movies a long time ago.

27. Which of the following statements is LEAST relevant in an informative essay about the history of World War II?

a. With the end of World War I came a rise in irredentist nationalism through Europe that was crucial in setting the stage for the Second World War.
b. Japan's attack on Pearl Harbor, Hawaii, was the decisive event that drew the United States into World War II.
c. World War II inspired a number of important novels, including Slaughterhouse-Five, The English Patient, and Catch 22.
d. World War II finally reached its conclusion when Japan formally surrendered on September 2, 1945.

28. Which of the following statements would provide the BEST transition to include in an essay about the history of baseball?

a. This sport introduced by European immigrants eventually would become known throughout the world as "The Great American Pastime."
b. The precise origins of baseball are difficult to trace, but it may have its roots in such British games as stoolball and cricket.
c. Baseball saw the formation of its first governing organization, the National Association of Base Ball Players, in 1857.
d. With its establishment in 1901, the American League became the first major rival to the National League.

29. Which of the following details from a narrative BEST would orient the reader?

a. A man gave my grandfather a job at his shop, and he remained there for several years.
b. Grandfather first set foot on American soil when he arrived at Ellis Island on March 2, 1910.
c. Grandfather's favorite saying was always, "A leopard never changes its spots."
d. Grandfather left his homeland to seek new opportunities across the sea.

30. Which of the following sentences BEST builds suspense in the narrative?

a. Suddenly, a bolt of lightning struck the great tree, and it came careening to the earth.
b. Inspector Ramirez examined the crime scene thoroughly but was unable to detect any useful clues.
c. The full moon shone down on the woods and cast strange shadows in the night.
d. Little did Natalie realize that her life was about to change in ways she'd never imagined.

31. Which of the following statements is MOST vivid?

a. Grey clouds indicated that a major storm was on the way, which could pose a threat to the tiny ship.
b. The boat rocked on the waves as the storm grew more intense, and the crew prepared for the difficulties to come.
c. Foaming sheets of black water flushed across the ship's deck, impelling the weary crew to scatter like spooked rabbits.
d. The storm finally came to an end as the storm clouds parted, the sun appeared, and the ship finally settled on the sea.

32. Which of the following statements BEST would introduce a fairy tale intended for new readers?

a. Princess Nafisa resided in a palatial estate in the clouds.
b. Albert skipped along the path; the witch observed him from her secret lair.
c. The malicious dragon awoke in its cave.
d. There once was a little frog named Reginald.

33. Read the following introduction from an essay about Mary Shelley.

Mary Shelley conceived of Dr. Frankenstein and the hideous monster he created, which helped the English novelist to make an immeasurable impact on literature and popular culture.

Which of the following statements most effectively revises this introduction?

a. English novelist Mary Shelley had an immeasurable impact on literature and popular culture when she conceived of Dr. Frankenstein and the hideous monster he created.
b. Dr. Frankenstein created a hideous monster, and they were conceived by English novelist Mary Shelley, who had an immeasurable impact on literature and popular culture.
c. English novelist Mary Shelley conceived of Dr. Frankenstein and the hideous monster he created and had an immeasurable impact on literature and popular culture.
d. Novelist Mary Shelley from England had an immeasurable impact on literature and popular culture when she conceived of Dr. Frankenstein and the hideous monster he created.

34. What is a benefit of publishing an article on the Internet instead of in a print magazine?

a. The Internet makes performing research for an article particularly easy.
b. If the article contains a mistake, it can be revised on the Internet; however, articles published in a magazine are permanent.
c. Publishing on the Internet requires greater knowledge of technology than magazine publishing.
d. With the increased use of the Internet, articles published on it earn the writer more money than articles published in magazines.

35. Which of the following answer choices offers the BEST way to find out how the film 2001: A Space Odyssey was regarded at the time of its release in 1968?

a. Attend a screening of 2001: A Space Odyssey.
b. Read original reviews of 2001: A Space Odyssey at the library.
c. Read the story on which 2001: A Space Odyssey was based.
d. Find a fan page for 2001: A Space Odyssey on the Internet.

36. Which of the following choices offers the MOST IMPORTANT benefit of composing a historical essay over an extended period of time rather than completing it in a single sitting and submitting it immediately?

a. Composing it over time allows the writer to incorporate any new developments on the subject.
b. Composing it over time ensures there will be no grammatical or spelling mistakes.
c. Composing it over time allows more opportunities for reflection and revision.
d. Composing it over time gives the writer time to take a class on composition.

37. Which of the following answer choices offers the BEST way to strengthen an oral argument?

a. Quote a source used to research the topic specifically.
b. Make simple generalizations about the topic.
c. Load the discussion with technical terminology.
d. Display a series of charts and illustrations.

38. Which of the following choices describes the BEST approach for organizing a team debate?

a. Allow the best debater on the team to do all the talking.
b. Choose an easy to follow debating order, such as alphabetical according to the team members' names.
c. Assign each member of the team a role in the debate that best uses his or her strengths.
d. Allow the first member who raises his or her hand to address the question asked.

39. When taking part in a debate, which of the following choices is the BEST way to address a false claim by the rival debater?

a. Immediately call the rival debater a liar in front of the audience.
b. Ignore the false claim because everyone is entitled to make a mistake or two.
c. Ask the rival debater to repeat his or her claim word for word.
d. Challenge the debater to provide evidence supporting his or her claim.

40. Which of the following choices describes a benefit of understanding both sides of an issue before debating it?

a. It will make you seem more understanding than your rival.
b. It will impress the audience watching the debate.
c. It will help you to understand that no one right position exists in any argument.
d. It will help you to anticipate your rival's arguments.

41. Why is it important to consult more than one source while researching a topic?

a. It will give you different ideas for wording your argument.
b. It will help you to validate or dismiss information.
c. It will show that many different ways exist to look at an issue.
d. It will prove you have taken your research seriously.

42. Which of the following statements is the LEAST effective line in a formal argument about health care?

a. It is imperative that all Americans have access to good, affordable health care.
b. According to the World Health Organization, a strong health care system goes hand-in-hand with a strong means of financing.
c. Nobody wants to pay too much money to get good health care because everyone thinks it's their right to get it for cheap.
d. Health care is an integral component of the economy, comprising nine percent of the gross national product in 2008, alone.

43. Read the following line from a speech arguing in favor of film preservation.

Film preservation may not seem like a particularly important pursuit, but it is more crucial than people often consider.

Which of the following is the BEST follow-up statement?

a. Films provide us with valuable perspectives of the eras in which they were created, so for reasons of historical importance, these documents should not be allowed to deteriorate.
b. Early film consisted of a nitrate base, and because this base was extremely flammable, many early films have been lost because they spontaneously caught fire.
c. Some of the great films that have benefitted from government-funded preservation are The Godfather, Citizen Kane, Star Wars, and The Wizard of Oz.
d. While I was growing up, my parents and I went to the movies every weekend, and this brought us closer together as a family.

44. Which of the following statements is NOT a benefit of using a video to illustrate a point in a speech?

a. It enhances the argument by actually showing your findings to the audience instead of merely talking about them.
b. It helps to maintain the audience's attention by providing an interesting new facet to the presentation.
c. It proves that you not only have skills as a public speaker but also as an accomplished filmmaker.
d. It enhances the reasoning in an argument by actually showing your findings and research to your audience.

45. Use of formal language would be LEAST essential when addressing which of the following audiences?

a. a board of directors
b. a grammar school class
c. a gathering of college professors
d. none of the above

46. Which version of the sentence does NOT contain any misspelled words?

a. The suspect remained detained while the police conducted their inquisiton.
b. The suspect remained detained while the police conducted their inquasition.
c. The suspect remained detained while the police conducted their inquesition.
d. The suspect remained detained while the police conducted their inquisition.

47. To temporarily postpone repayment of a loan is to

a. decry
b. defer
c. differ
d. debtor

48. Which version of the sentence is written correctly?

a. The two-year-old was just learning how to walk.
b. The two-year old was just learning how to walk.
c. The two year-old was just learning how to walk.
d. The two year old was just learning how to walk.

49. Which of the following versions of the sentence is best??

a. Because she wanted to reduce unnecessary waste, Cicily decided to have the television repaired instead of buying a new one.
b. Cicily decided to have the television repaired because she wanted to reduce unnecessary waste instead of buying a new one.
c. Cicily decided to have, because she wanted to reduce unnecessary waste, the television repaired instead of buying a new one.
d. Because Cicily decided to have the television repaired instead of buying a new one she wanted to reduce unnecessary waste.

50. Which of the following versions of the sentence is best?

a. The audience at the poetry reading filled few seats than the one at the concert last week.
b. The audience at the poetry reading filled less seats than the one at the concert last week.
c. The audience at the poetry reading filled fewer seats than the one at the concert last week.
d. The audience at the poetry reading filled lesser seats than the one at the concert last week.

51. The melody in that pop song is reminiscent of the one Beethoven used in the first movement of his ninth symphony?

Based on how it is used in the sentence, the word <u>reminiscent</u> means

a. superior
b. suggestive
c. situated
d. synonymous

52. Which of the following is the best way to write the sentence?

a. Any person who uses his or her cell phone in a movie theater has little respect for the other audience members.
b. Any person who uses their cell phone in a movie theater has little respect for the other audience members.
c. Any person who uses its cell phone in a movie theater has little respect for the other audience members.
d. Any person who uses his cell phone in a movie theater has little respect for the other audience members.

53. Which of the following versions of the sentence is best?

a. To repeat ideas in an essay unnecessarily is to commit the mistake of redundant.
b. To repeat ideas in an essay unnecessarily is to commit the mistake of redundantly.
c. To repeat ideas in an essay unnecessarily is to commit the mistake of redundancy.
d. To repeat ideas in an essay unnecessarily is to commit the mistake of redundance.

54. Which version of the sentence is written correctly?

a. We stopped for extended visits in Indiana, Kansas, Nevada and California during our cross country trip.
b. We stopped for extended visits, in Indiana, Kansas, Nevada and California during our cross-country trip.
c. We stopped for extended visits in Indiana, Kansas, Nevada and California, during our cross-country trip.
d. We stopped for extended visits in Indiana, Kansas, Nevada, and California during our cross-country trip.

55. According to Merriam-Webster's Dictionary, what is the correct pronunciation of the word "impromptu?"

a. \im-promp-too
b. \imp-römp-tu
c. \im-'präm(p)-(,)tü
d. \im-prömpt-ü

56. As used in the sentence, "Julie and I made tentative plans to go to the park because she might have to study that day," what does the word <u>tentative</u> mean?

a. specific
b. uncertain
c. absolute
d. unlikely

57. William Shakespeare's character Hamlet said, "I must be cruel only to be kind." What did Hamlet most likely mean?

a. Cruelty and kindness can be indistinguishable; recognizing the difference is confusing.
b. Sometimes a person must perform a cruel act that will have positive effects in the long run.
c. The only way to achieve true kindness is through acts that may seem cruel at first.
d. Despite what most people believe, cruelty and kindness share the same meaning.

58. To place something or someone in peril is to

a. jubilate.
b. juxtapose.
c. jocular.
d. jeopardize.

Answers and Explanations

1. D: The "slings and arrows of outrageous fortune" are the terrible circumstances of bad luck. When Hamlet considers taking "arms against" these "troubles" by ending them, he is considering killing himself. Although his line about "the sleep of death" also is fixated on death, he merely is wondering what happens and what people might think or "dream" about in death.

2. B: Hamlet's fear of the unknown, "the undiscovered country," prevents him from resolving to kill himself. Death is an unknown, and he says his fear of it "makes cowards of us all." He seems to resolve not to take an action as drastic as killing himself by the end of his monologue, and the passage offers no evidence that he will reverse this issue once Ophelia leaves the scene.

3. C: Interacting with loved ones can make a person feel alive, so cutting off such interaction can constitute a sort of self-imposed death, even if such death is not literal. However, saying that interacting with loved ones is the only thing that makes life worth living is an absolute, and absolutes rarely are true for all people. Although Hamlet seems to have little regard for Ophelia in this excerpt, he may not be treating her this way because he actually has little regard for her.

4. A: Someone who had only moments ago been contemplating killing himself probably is not well, as Hamlet says when Ophelia asks how he is doing ("How does your honour for this many a day?"). Therefore, Hamlet's response is ironic. No evidence in this excerpt supports the conclusion that Hamlet is conceited or that he does not believe Ophelia is a pretty lady. Hamlet does say he did not give gifts to Ophelia, but untruthful statements are not inherently ironic.

5. C: Ultimately, Hamlet decides not to kill himself, which means he has resolved not to take an active role in changing his situation. Willy resolves to kill himself and goes through with it. If he believed that bad situations always work themselves out in the end, he would not have taken the decisive yet tragic action of taking his own life.

6. A: Emma's life had been marked by the comfort of consistency, a close relationship with Miss Taylor, and the knowledge she tended to get her own way. Miss Taylor's marriage upsets that comfort and consistency because a major aspect of Emma's life will change. Emma is afraid her intellect will be stifled without Miss Taylor, so she does not approach the change as an opportunity for possible intellectual growth.

7. D: The author uses words such as comfortable and happy to describe Emma's first twenty-one years. During this time, little vexed her. Based on this context, you can conclude that *vex* has the opposite meaning of words such as comfortable and happy. The answer choice most different from these positive words is displease.

8. C: The author states that Emma possesses the "power of having rather too much her own way," and instead of feeling happy for her recently married friend, she feels sorry for herself. These descriptions characterize Emma as selfish. Emma may consider herself unfortunate following Miss Taylor's marriage, but a lifetime of privilege and having her own way hardly makes her an unfortunate character. While Emma may indeed prove to be devious, this excerpt offers no evidence of deviousness. Although Emma seems to value intellectual interaction, nothing in the excerpt implies that she is particularly studious.

9. B: A product of upper-class privilege, Emma has grown accustomed always to getting her way. When Miss Taylor's marriage disrupts this aspect of her life, Emma cannot deal with the situation in a mature fashion and instead sinks into self-pity and sorrow. Although Emma cannot enjoy Miss

Taylor's happiness upon her wedding because Emma is so wrapped up in her own feelings, this does not mean she feels neither kindness nor love for her friend.

10. B: The color black is often used figuratively to suggest badness. Emma is sad about Miss Taylor's wedding, and enduring the event has become nothing more than "black work" to her. Perhaps she pretends she is happy about the wedding, but no evidence in this excerpt suggests this conclusion. In addition, no evidence in the excerpt suggests that Emma organized the wedding. The author does not use "black" as a literal color in this excerpt, and no evidence in the excerpt suggests the wedding party wears black clothing.

11. D: By beginning his argument with an immediate criticism of the existing federal government, he immediately portrays it as a system in need of improvement. By presenting the government's inefficacy in no uncertain terms, Hamilton assumes the reader will take his claim at face value and be convinced of his subsequent argument for improvements. Hamilton only criticizes the federal government explicitly; he does not criticize the Constitution.

12. A: By addressing the reader directly and uniting himself with the reader by using words such as "we," Hamilton is establishing a sense of agreement between himself and the reader. By doing so he wants the reader to believe he and the reader share the same desires for and concerns about America. The first-person point of view does not necessarily establish a friendly or informal tone.

13. C: Alexander Hamilton describes his opponents as loud and bitter in this sentence. Such words suggest a lack of rationality, self-control, and kindness. This word usage almost represents an attempt to portray his political opponents as less than human. Hamilton is seeking to strengthen his argument by suggesting those oppose his argument are angry and irrational.

14. B: In paragraph 3, Alexander Hamilton attacks politicians who fear any change resulting from the Constitution that might diminish their power. Although this attack may be central to his argument, Hamilton does not want to leave the reader with the bitter feeling that Hamilton's sole reason for writing is to attack his opponents. Ironically, he then continues his attacks for the remainder of the excerpt.

15. A: According to the writer, a tyrant would start by pretending to be submissive to the will of the people (that is, paying court to the people) to gain popularity, then abuse his or her newfound power. Based on this context, you can conclude that "obsequious" and "submissive" share the same meaning.

16. B: In the opening paragraph of his second inaugural address, Lincoln discusses his first address, describing how the first actions in the coming Civil War were just beginning to take place. The country had suffered much since then as the war got underway and continued throughout his first term as president. This change in the nation inspired the plea for an end to the hostilities that dominates his second inaugural address.

17. C: Lincoln believed that the South was wrong for making war by trying to secede from the Union, and the North was right for trying to maintain the Union by refusing to accept the hostile action. This quote shows he believed the actions of the North were more justifiable than those of the South.

18. A: Lincoln states that "if God wills that it [the war] continue ... until every drop of blood drawn with the lash shall be paid by another drawn with the sword, as was said three thousand years ago, so still it must be said 'the judgments of the Lord are true and righteous altogether.'" This statement indicates Lincoln's belief that the war was a product of God's will.

19. D: Lincoln delivered his Second Inaugural Address after a time of great hardship for the United States: the Civil War. His plea for the country's resolution of its severe problems must have been an emotional experience for the president, and his voice must have conveyed this emotionality as he read the speech. As a result, reading the document online could not have quite the same emotional impact as hearing it in person.

20. C: Lincoln's final paragraph issues a plea for "malice toward none, with charity for all." This statement represents an attempt to heal the pain that existed between the North and South during the Civil War. Lincoln wants the United States to reunite and move on from the war as a solid, individual, caring nation.

21. C: All of these are good sources to use while developing a position on civil rights; nonetheless, first you must first familiarize yourself with an overview of the issue. A history textbook probably would be the most comprehensive and the least affected by personal opinion. Speeches, interviews, and blogs are great next steps in the research process, but these choices may prove too subjective to provide a necessary overview of the issue.

22. B: The key to an effective concluding statement is a concise summary of the argument's main points. Such a conclusion leaves the opponent and audience with a clear and organized understanding of the argument. The introduction of new points, or a detail added merely to lighten mood, would weaken the argument by straying off point at the last minute. Introducing contradictory perspectives completely would work against the argument's effectiveness.

23. A: The first sentence introduces an argument against complete freedom of speech. The second sentence makes an argument in favor of it. The second argument opposes the first one, so the two sentences should be linked with the adverb "however." "Therefore" and "so" would be used only if the sentences supported each other.

24. D: Global environmental protection relates to measures that expand beyond a single neighborhood, forest, or area that might have been damaged by illegal garbage dumping. Scientifically supported statistics about environmental damage throughout the world addresses the global impact of pollution and is not as subjective as a personal story or editorial.

25. D: This statement mentions the death of William Shakespeare, effectively indicating his end. It also refers to the importance and continued relevance of his work in the years to come, which is integral to any general essay about the playwright. This statement offers a stronger conclusion to an essay on William Shakespeare than stopping short with the cause and date of his death. In addition, this choice does not stray from an authoritative tone by presenting personal opinion about Shakespeare's best play or a random detail about the theaters that staged his work.

26. B: One of the keys to creating a convincing essay is the establishment of a formal tone. Accordingly, the writer can accomplish such a tone through tight structure, strong grammar, and objectivity. The assertion that "few filmmakers had as far-reaching effect on the medium as Alfred Hitchcock" is an indisputable fact, so it establishes objectivity. Comments about the writer's personal favorite Hitchcock movies are subjective. Using informal words such as "awesome" undermine the formal tone required by a convincing essay.

27. C: A list of important novels inspired by World War II is less relevant to an essay about the war than facts about its early causes, its decisive moments, and its conclusion. A strong essay should remain on topic without unnecessary tangents. If the topic were "World War II novels," this detail would be perfectly relevant, but it probably has no place in a general essay about the war.

28. A: By presenting two distinct yet related ideas, this sentence provides a clear transition between baseball's European origins and its coming importance as the United States' national sport. The other sentences present fine details, but they all focus on a single idea, so they do not provide good transitions between two ideas.

29. B: This statement orients the reader with precise details about character (the narrator's grandfather), place (Ellis Island), and time (March 2, 1910). The other sentences present some orienting information, yet none set the scene nearly as thoroughly.

30. D: Suspense is created with the suggestion of major details that have yet to come. This sentence creates suspense by suggesting the coming of a major event (a big change in Natalie's life) without yet revealing the exact nature of the major event. The reader now wants to know what the change might entail. The falling of a tree by lightning is more the outcome of suspense rather than suspense, itself.

31. C: All of these sentences are clear and somewhat descriptive, but only choice C fashions a completely vivid picture of the scene. Rather than merely writing something such as "The waves hit the ship and the crew ran away," the writer describes the waves as "foaming sheets of black water" and uses a simile comparing the crew to spooked rabbits.

32. D: New readers require brief, simply constructed, and easily understood sentences. They would be confused by overly advanced vocabulary (resided, palatial, malicious, etc.) or by a compound sentence linked with a semicolon.

33. A: This sentence offers the most effective revision. The syntax is clearer than the other answer choices. The writer achieves maximum impact by holding Mary Shelley's achievement, the creation of Dr. Frankenstein and his hideous monster in her novel *Frankenstein*, for the end of the sentence.

34. B: When an article appears in print, it no longer can be revised. If it contains an error, the best a magazine can do is publish a correction in a future issue. Articles on the Internet can be revised easily at any time. While the Internet makes research easier, researching and publishing are not the same things. The idea that publishing requires greater knowledge of technology is not really a benefit. More often than not, writers are not paid at all for work posted on the Internet, so it is untrue that they always earn more money by publishing on the Internet than in print magazines.

35. B: The very best way to research initial critical opinion of anything is to locate vintage reviews of it in periodicals at the library. Watching the film or reading the story on which the film was based will reveal nothing about critical opinion of it. A fan page on the Internet may very well include vintage reviews, but such an assumption is not automatically true. If the page does include reprints of vintage reviews, it is impossible to know if they were reprinted accurately without consulting the original sources.

36. C: Dashing off an essay in a single sitting is a good way to get it over with, but such a method does not ensure effective writing. Taking ones time allows more opportunities to reread and rewrite the piece. A writer probably should not expect any major new developments to occur while writing about a subject that took place in the past. While the opportunities for revision that time allows may result in an essay free of errors, this is not guaranteed.

37. A: A good way to prove an argument's central point is to support it with specific evidence from your research, thereby indicating your central point as based on more than mere subjective opinion. This can be accomplished simply by quoting supporting evidence from a reliable source. Technical terminology may only strengthen your argument if addressing an audience that would

understand such terminology. As a result, using technical terminology is not a sure way to strengthen an argument. Charts and illustrations may be relevant only to certain topics, so choice D is not the best answer, either.

38. C: Different people have different strengths. A strong debate team capitalizes on its members' strengths by having them address questions that specifically utilize those strengths. Allowing the best debater to dominate may be a good strategy for winning, but such an approach hardly is fair to every member of the team. Alphabetical order and allowing the first responder to address a question makes no use of the team members' individual strengths.

39. D: Responding to a rival swiftly yet respectfully is a key to conducting a strong debate. Such a response would be accomplished not by using insults such as "liar," but by respectfully asking the rival to support his or her claim with reliable evidence. If the claim truly is false, the rival will not be able to support it, and you will gain the upper hand in the debate.

40. D: Anticipating your rival's arguments is a key to conducting a strong debate. Having an idea of what your rival may say will help you prepare counter-arguments before the debate. While your knowledge may make you seem more understanding or impress your audience, neither will really strengthen your argument.

41. B: Even printed sources can be wrong sometimes. By cross-referencing your research and consulting more than one source, you can find out whether a source is reliable. Such effort is particularly important when conducting Internet research, since a good deal of information on the Internet is incorrect. Although consulting more than one source may give you different ideas of how to word your argument or show that many different ways to look at an issue, these reasons are not quite as important as validating and dismissing information.

42. C: Strong statements stated clearly are keys to a strong argument. This statement is neither strong nor clear. It contains an unsupported generalization ("everyone thinks it's their right to get it for cheap") and saying both this and "Nobody wants to pay too much money to get good health" is redundant. The word choice and syntax also are sloppy and informal.

43. A: The first line sets up the ideas that film preservation is of grand importance. This follow-up statement supports this claim of importance by explaining films' historical significance and comparing their deterioration to the destruction of historical documents. The other answer choices may be relevant in an argument in favor of film preservation, but they are not particularly strong follow-ups to the statement in the question.

44. C: Showing off your filmmaking skills is not really essential to most speeches. Besides, the question does not state that you are the one who makes the video. The other answer choices offer strong arguments for using video evidence to enhance an oral presentation.

45. B: Young people will respond to and better comprehend informal, friendly speech. However, you would not want to be too informal when addressing an educated gathering of college professors or a professional board of directors. Informal speech likely would weaken addresses made before such audiences.

46. D: Although the word inquisition means a prolonged process of questioning, it is not spelled with an <e>, as is question. The correct spelling uses an <i>, as in inquire.

47. B: To defer is to temporarily put off, postpone, or delay an action. To defer a loan is to postpone its repayment with the intention of resuming repayments in the future. To decry means to criticize. To differ means to vary or disagree. Debtor is a noun meaning someone who owes a debt.

48. A: Adjective phrases consisting of more than one word (compound modifiers) should be hyphenated, even if the person, place, or thing they're describing is only implied. The word child is only implied in this sentence, but the adjective phrase describing it—"two-year-old"—still needs to be fully hyphenated in order for it to be correct.

49. A: The syntax of this sentence is correct. It uses a comma to offset the subordinate clause ("Because she wanted to reduce unnecessary waste") from the independent clause ("Cicily decided to have the television repaired instead of buying a new one"). Placing the independent clause, which is the most important idea in the sentence, at the end for emphasis also makes the sentence stronger.

50. C: When comparing things that can be counted, the correct adjective to use is fewer. The word less refers to anything that cannot be counted (i.e. less room, less confidence, etc.). Since seats are items that can be counted, the word fewer is correct in this sentence.

51. B: The sentence compares the melody of a pop song to that of the first movement in Beethoven's ninth symphony. Therefore, concluding that they probably are similar is logical. The pop song reminds the speaker of the Beethoven piece, which means the pop song suggests the melody of the Beethoven piece. Reminiscent and suggestive are synonyms in this context.

52. A: Using the male-pronoun, such as "his," once was proper when referring to an unspecified person. However, this practice is now considered gender biased, as it does not take the possibility that the person could be female into account. Today the best way to indicate an unspecified person is with pronoun phrases that take both genders into account, such "his or her," "he or she," or "him or her."

53. C: In the context of this sentence, the word redundant should appear in its noun form, which is redundancy (meaning "unnecessary repetition"). Redundant is an adjective, and redundantly is an adverb. Redundance is a nonstandard variant of redundancy and is not widely accepted.

54. D: The comma that comes after the next-to-last item in a list (in this case, Nevada) is called the serial comma. It is okay to include it (choice D) or not (the other three choices). But choices B and C each include an extra comma where it does not belong. Choice A misses the essential hyphen that should join the adjective phrase *cross-country*.

55. C: The Merriam-Webster's Dictionary states that \im-'präm(p)-(,)tü is the correct pronunciation of the word "impromptu." This pronunciation indicates that the o is pronounced ä, which is an open vowel that sounds like "ah," the p is optional, and the ü is pronounced "oo."

56. B: Julie may have to study on the day she and the speaker consider going to the park, which means their plans are uncertain. The plans might happen, but they also might not happen. Based on this context, you can conclude that the word tentative means "uncertain." Because the speaker does not indicate that either the plan to go to the park or the possibility Julie may have to study is more likely, unlikely is not the best answer choice.

57. B: Hamlet's line is a paradox: a figurative expression that seems to contradict itself yet makes sense. In Shakespeare's play, Hamlet feels responsible for eliminating corruption in the Danish

court, and he believes the only way to achieve this goal is by killing certain people. So his "cruel" acts (murder) he will have "kind" results (the elimination of corruption).

58. D: The noun jeopardy is a synonym of peril. To jeopardize is a verb meaning to place something or someone in peril or danger. Jubilate means to express joy. Juxtapose means to place side by side. Jocular is an adjective meaning humorous or witty.

Practice Test #2

Practice Questions

QUESTIONS 1-5 PERTAIN TO THE FOLLOWING EXCERPT.

Excerpt from Wuthering Heights

By Emily Brontë

Chapter 1

1801.—I have just returned from a visit to my landlord—the solitary neighbour that I shall be troubled with. This is certainly a beautiful country! In all England, I do not believe that I could have fixed on a situation so completely removed from the stir of society. A perfect misanthropist's heaven: and Mr. Heathcliff and I are such a suitable pair to divide the desolation between us. A capital fellow! He little imagined how my heart warmed towards him when I beheld his black eyes withdraw so suspiciously under their brows, as I rode up, and when his fingers sheltered themselves, with a jealous resolution, still further in his waistcoat, as I announced my name.

"Mr. Heathcliff?" I said. A nod was the answer.

"Mr. Lockwood, your new tenant, sir. I do myself the honour of calling as soon as possible after my arrival, to express the hope that I have not inconvenienced you by my perseverance in soliciting the occupation of Thrushcross Grange: I heard yesterday you had had some thoughts—"

"Thrushcross Grange is my own, sir," he interrupted, wincing. "I should not allow any one to inconvenience me, if I could hinder it—walk in!"

The "walk in" was uttered with closed teeth, and expressed the sentiment, "Go to the Deuce:" even the gate over which he leant manifested no sympathizing movement to the words; and I think that circumstance determined me to accept the invitation: I felt interested in a man who seemed more exaggeratedly reserved than myself.

When he saw my horse's breast fairly pushing the barrier, he did put out his hand to unchain it, and then sullenly preceded me up the causeway, calling, as we entered the court—"Joseph, take Mr. Lockwood's horse; and bring up some wine."

"Here we have the whole establishment of domestics, I suppose," was the reflection suggested by this compound order. "No wonder the grass grows up between the flags, and cattle are the only hedge-cutters."

Joseph was an elderly, nay, an old man: very old, perhaps, though hale and sinewy. "The Lord help us!" he soliloquized in an undertone of peevish displeasure, while relieving me of my horse: looking, meantime, in my face so sourly that I charitably conjectured he must have need of divine aid to digest his dinner, and his pious ejaculation had no reference to my unexpected advent.

Wuthering Heights is the name of Mr. Heathcliff's dwelling. "Wuthering" being a significant provincial adjective, descriptive of the atmospheric tumult to which its station is exposed in stormy weather. Pure, bracing ventilation they must have up there at all times, indeed: one may guess the power of the north wind blowing over the edge, by the excessive slant of a few stunted firs at the end of the house; and by a range of gaunt thorns all stretching their limbs one way, as if craving alms of the sun. Happily, the architect had foresight to build it strong: the narrow windows are deeply set in the wall, and the corners defended with large jutting stones.

Before passing the threshold, I paused to admire a quantity of grotesque carving lavished over the front, and especially about the principal door; above which, among a wilderness of crumbling griffins and shameless little boys, I detected the date "1500," and the name "Hareton Earnshaw.'" I would have made a few comments, and requested a short history of the place from the surly owner; but his attitude at the door appeared to demand my speedy entrance, or complete departure, and I had no desire to aggravate his impatience previous to inspecting the penetralium.

1. What is the author's purpose in describing Wuthering Heights in such detail?

a. to explain why Mr. Lockwood is so delighted by the house
b. to prove that Heathcliff is a misanthrope
c. to show how all houses looked in the 1500s
d. to establish a strange and foreboding tone

2. Which line from the excerpt helps establish a somewhat sarcastic tone?

a. ... Mr. Heathcliff and I are such a suitable pair to divide the desolation between us.
b. ... I charitably conjectured he must have need of divine aid to digest his dinner...
c. ... the narrow windows are deeply set in the wall, and the corners defended with large jutting stones.
d. ... his attitude at the door appeared to demand my speedy entrance...

3. As it is used in paragraph 8, what does the word bracing mean?

a. supporting
b. bracketing
c. staying.
d. invigorating

4. What does Heathcliff mean when he says, "cattle are the only hedge-cutters"?

a. Heathcliff is mad and believes his cattle are capable of gardening.
b. Heathcliff is irritated by how the cattle destroy the vegetation on his property.
c. The only way his property will be landscaped is if cattle decide to eat the hedges.
d. The hedges that grow on Heathcliff's property are particularly delicious to cattle.

5. Although now regarded as a classic, Wuthering Heights received some harsh reviews when published in 1847. Based on this excerpt, what might have been one of the most common criticisms?

a. The characters are not particularly likable.
b. Emily Bronte misuses language.
c. The plot is completely unoriginal.
d. Emily Bronte fails to describe the characters.

QUESTIONS 6-10 PERTAIN TO THE FOLLOWING EXCERPT.

Excerpt from Act 1, Scene 1 of A Midsummer Night's Dream

By William Shakespeare

Enter EGEUS, HERMIA, LYSANDER, and DEMETRIUS

EGEUS: Happy be Theseus, our renowned duke!

THESEUS: Thanks, good Egeus: what's the news with thee?

EGEUS: Full of vexation come I, with complaint

Against my child, my daughter Hermia.

Stand forth, Demetrius. My noble lord,

This man hath my consent to marry her.

Stand forth, Lysander: and my gracious duke,

This man hath bewitch'd the bosom of my child;

Thou, thou, Lysander, thou hast given her rhymes,

And interchanged love-tokens with my child:

Thou hast by moonlight at her window sung,

With feigning voice verses of feigning love,

And stolen the impression of her fantasy

With bracelets of thy hair, rings, gawds, conceits,

Knacks, trifles, nosegays, sweetmeats, messengers

Of strong prevailment in unharden'd youth:

With cunning hast thou filch'd my daughter's heart,

Turn'd her obedience, which is due to me,

To stubborn harshness: and, my gracious duke,

Be it so she; will not here before your grace

Consent to marry with Demetrius,

I beg the ancient privilege of Athens,

As she is mine, I may dispose of her:

Which shall be either to this gentleman

Or to her death, according to our law

Immediately provided in that case.

THESEUS: What say you, Hermia? be advised fair maid:

To you your father should be as a god;

One that composed your beauties, yea, and one

To whom you are but as a form in wax

By him imprinted and within his power

To leave the figure or disfigure it.

Demetrius is a worthy gentleman.

HERMIA: So is Lysander.

THESEUS: In himself he is;

But in this kind, wanting your father's voice,

The other must be held the worthier.

HERMIA: I would my father look'd but with my eyes.

THESEUS: Rather your eyes must with his judgment look.

HERMIA: I do entreat your grace to pardon me.

I know not by what power I am made bold,

Nor how it may concern my modesty,

In such a presence here to plead my thoughts;

But I beseech your grace that I may know

The worst that may befall me in this case,

If I refuse to wed Demetrius.

THESEUS: Either to die the death or to abjure

For ever the society of men.

Therefore, fair Hermia, question your desires;

Know of your youth, examine well your blood,

Whether, if you yield not to your father's choice,

You can endure the livery of a nun,

For aye to be in shady cloister mew'd,

To live a barren sister all your life,

Chanting faint hymns to the cold fruitless moon.

Thrice-blessed they that master so their blood,

To undergo such maiden pilgrimage;

But earthlier happy is the rose distill'd,

Than that which withering on the virgin thorn

Grows, lives and dies in single blessedness.

HERMIA: So will I grow, so live, so die, my lord,

Ere I will my virgin patent up

Unto his lordship, whose unwished yoke

My soul consents not to give sovereignty.

THESEUS: Take time to pause; and, by the nest new moon--

The sealing-day betwixt my love and me,

For everlasting bond of fellowship--

Upon that day either prepare to die

For disobedience to your father's will,

Or else to wed Demetrius, as he would;

Or on Diana's altar to protest

For aye austerity and single life.

DEMETRIUS: Relent, sweet Hermia: and, Lysander, yield

Thy crazed title to my certain right.

LYSANDER: You have her father's love, Demetrius;

Let me have Hermia's: do you marry him.

EGEUS: Scornful Lysander! true, he hath my love,

And what is mine my love shall render him.

And she is mine, and all my right of her

I do estate unto Demetrius.

LYSANDER: I am, my lord, as well derived as he,

As well possess'd; my love is more than his;

My fortunes every way as fairly rank'd,

If not with vantage, as Demetrius';

And, which is more than all these boasts can be,

I am beloved of beauteous Hermia:

Why should not I then prosecute my right?

Demetrius, I'll avouch it to his head,

Made love to Nedar's daughter, Helena,

And won her soul; and she, sweet lady, dotes,

Devoutly dotes, dotes in idolatry,

Upon this spotted and inconstant man.

THESEUS: I must confess that I have heard so much,

And with Demetrius thought to have spoke thereof;

But, being over-full of self-affairs,

My mind did lose it. But, Demetrius, come;

And come, Egeus; you shall go with me,

I have some private schooling for you both.

For you, fair Hermia, look you arm yourself

To fit your fancies to your father's will;

Or else the law of Athens yields you up--

Which by no means we may extenuate--

To death, or to a vow of single life.

Come, my Hippolyta: what cheer, my love?

Demetrius and Egeus, go along:

I must employ you in some business

Against our nuptial and confer with you

Of something nearly that concerns yourselves.

EGEUS: With duty and desire we follow you.

Exeunt all but LYSANDER and HERMIA

6. At the end of this excerpt, everyone exits except for Lysander and Hermia. Why might the writer allow these two characters to remain in the scene together?

a. Lysander and Hermia decide to end their relationship during the excerpt and will say their final goodbyes when left alone together.
b. Lysander and Hermia are not included in Theseus's request that Demetrious, Egeus, and Hippolyta follow him elsewhere.
c. Lysander and Hermia are the two main characters of the play and therefore are expected to share a number of scenes together.
d. Lysander and Hermia are in love and will discuss how their relationship will proceed after the other characters leave.

7. Which of the following does Egeus NOT accuse Lysander of doing?

a. giving gifts to Hermia
b. singing to Hermia
c. writing poetry for Hermia
d. painting a portrait of Hermia

8. A Midsummer Night's Dream deals with the themes of true love and mismatched relationships. In what way are these themes paralleled in Lysander and Demetrius?

a. Both love women who do not love them.
b. Both love women they know are not right for them.
c. Both love women they are not supposed to marry.
d. Both love women who are unaware of the men who love them.

9. Which line from the excerpt proves Hermia's willingness to pursue her relationship with Lysander no matter the cost?

a. I beseech your grace that I may know / The worst that may befall me in this case, / If I refuse to wed Demetrius
b. I do entreat your grace to pardon me. / I know not by what power I am made bold, / Nor how it may concern my modesty
c. Know of your youth, examine well your blood, / Whether, if you yield not to your father's choice, / You can endure the livery of a nun
d. Unto his lordship, whose unwished yoke / My soul consents not to give sovereignty

10. Nathaniel Hawthorne's novel The Scarlett Letter deals with a romantic relationship criticized because the woman loves a man who is married to someone else. How does this differ from the situation in this excerpt from A Midsummer Night's Dream?

a. Hermia and Lysander do not actually love each other.
b. Hermia and Lysander are only involved with each other.
c. Hermia and Demetrious are not yet married.
d. Hermia and Demetrious are being kept apart by her father.

QUESTIONS 11-15 PERTAIN TO THE FOLLOWING EXCERPT.

The United States Bill of Rights

Article I. After the first enumeration required by the first article of the Constitution, there shall be one representative for every thirty thousand, until the number shall amount to one hundred, after which the proportion shall be so regulated by

Congress, that there shall not be less than one hundred representatives, nor less than one representative for every forty thousand persons, until the number of representatives shall amount to two hundred, after which the proportion shall be so regulated by Congress, that there shall not be less than two hundred representatives, nor more than one representative for every fifty thousand.

Article II. No law varying the compensation for services of the senators and representatives shall take effect, until an election of representatives shall have intervened.

Article III. Congress shall make no law respecting an establishment of religion, or prohibiting the free exercise thereof, or abridging the freedom of speech, or of the press, or the right of the people peaceably to assemble, and to petition the government for a redress of grievances.

Article IV. A well-regulated militia being necessary to the security of a free state, the right of the people to keep and bear arms shall not be infringed.

Article V. No soldier shall, in time of peace, be quartered in any house without the consent of the owner, nor in time of war, but in a manner prescribed by law.

Article VI. The right of the people to be secure in their persons, houses, papers, effects, against unreasonable searches and seizures, shall not be violated; and no warrants shall issue, but upon principal cause, supported by oath or affirmation, and particularly describing the place to be searched, and the persons or things to be seized.

Article VII. No person shall be held to answer for a capital or otherwise infamous crime, unless on a presentment or indictment of a grand jury, except in cases arising in the land or naval forces, or in the militia when in actual service, in time of war or public danger; nor shall any person be subject, for the same offence, to be twice put in jeopardy of life or limb; nor shall be compelled, in any criminal case, to be a witness against himself; nor be deprived of life, liberty, or property, without due process of law; nor shall private property be taken for public use without just compensation.

Article VIII. In all criminal prosecutions, the accused shall enjoy the right of a speedy and public trial, by an impartial jury of the state and district wherein the crime shall have been committed, which district shall have been previously ascertained by law; and to be informed of the nature and cause of the accusation; to be confronted with the witnesses against him; to have compulsory process for obtaining witnesses in his favor; and to have the assistance of counsel for his defense.

Article IX. In suits at common law, where the value in controversy shall exceed twenty dollars, the right of trial by jury shall be preserved, and no fact tried by a jury shall be otherwise reexamined, in any court of the United States, than according to the rules in common law.

Article X. Excessive bail shall not be required, nor excessive fines imposed, nor cruel and unusual punishments inflicted.

Article XI. The enumeration, in the Constitution, of certain rights, shall not be construed to deny or disparage others retained by the people.

Article XII. The powers not delegated to the United States by the Constitution, nor prohibited by it to the states, are reserved to the states, respectively, or to the people.

11. What is a purpose of Article III?

a. placing limitations on harmful speech
b. maintaining the separation of church and state
c. listing common grievances against the government
d. encouraging people to assemble peaceably

12. Which Article protects privacy and ownership?

a. Article II
b. Article III
c. Article IV
d. Article V

13. What idea recurs in Articles VI through XI?

a. the protection of the property and rights of those accused of committing a crime
b. the protection of the victims and the perpetrators of violent crimes
c. the insurance that criminal trials are conducted efficiently and quickly
d. the insurance that property is not illegally seized or searched

14. Which of the following sources would prove best to consult if disputing the contents of the Bill of Rights?

a. someone considered an expert on the document
b. a reprint of the document in a school textbook
c. a photo of the document on the Internet
d. the original documents

15. Why is the Bill of Rights divided into brief sections?

a. to emphasize the fluidness of its prose
b. to draw attention to its most important sections
c. to make it well organized and clear
d. to place the most important sections first

QUESTIONS 16-20 PERTAIN TO THE FOLLOWING EXCERPT.

Excerpt from President Woodrow Wilson's 1919 Address in Favor of the League of Nations

It gives me pleasure to add to this formal reading of the result of our labors that the character of the discussion, which occurred at the sittings of the commission was not only of the most constructive but of the most encouraging sort. It was obvious throughout our discussions that, although there were subjects upon which there were individual differences of judgment with regard to the method by which our objects should be obtained, there was practically at no point any serious differences of opinion or motive as to the objects which we were seeking.

Indeed, while these debates were not made the opportunity for the expression of enthusiasm and sentiments, I think the other members of the commission will agree with me that there was an undertone of high respect and of enthusiasm for the thing we were trying to do which was heartening throughout everything.

Because we felt that in a way this conference did entrust into us the expression of one of its highest and most important purposes, to see to it that the concord of the world in the future with regard to the objects of justice should not be subject to doubt or uncertainty; that the cooperation of the great body of nations should be assured in the maintenance of peace upon terms of honor and of international obligations.

The compulsion of that task was constantly upon us, and at no point was there shown the slightest desire to do anything but suggest the best means to accomplish that great object. There is very great significance, therefore, in the fact that the result was reached unanimously.

Fourteen nations were represented, among them all of those powers which for convenience we have called the Great Powers, and among the rest a representation of the greatest variety of circumstances and interests. So that I think we are justified in saying that the significance of the result, therefore, has the deepest of all meanings, the union of wills in a common purpose, a union of wills which cannot be resisted and which, I dare say, no nation will run the risk of attempting to resist.

Now, as to the character of the document. While it has consumed some time to read this document, I think you will see at once that it is very simple, and in nothing so simple as in the structure which it suggests for a league of nations, a body of delegates, an executive council, and a permanent secretariat.

When it came to the question of determining the character of the representation in the Body of Delegates, we were all aware of a feeling which is current throughout the world.

Inasmuch as I am stating it in the presence of the official representatives of the various governments here present, including myself, I may say that there is a universal feeling that the world cannot rest satisfied with merely official guidance. There has reached us through many channels the feeling that if the deliberating body of the League of Nations was merely to be a body of officials representing the various governments, the peoples of the world would not be sure that some of the mistakes which preoccupied officials had admittedly made might not be repeated.

It was impossible to conceive a method or an assembly so large and various as to be really representative of the great body of the peoples of the world, because, as I roughly reckon it, we represent as we sit around this table more than 1.2 billion people.

You cannot have a representative assembly of 1.2 billion people, but if you leave it to each government to have, if it pleases, one or two or three representatives, though only with a single vote, it may vary its representation from time to time, not only, but it may (originate) the choice of its several representatives [wireless here unintelligible.

Therefore we thought that this was a proper and a very prudent concession to the practically universal opinion of plain men everywhere that they wanted the door left open to a variety of representation, instead of being confined to a single official body with which they could or might not find themselves in sympathy.

And you will notice that this body has unlimited rights of discussion. I mean of discussion of anything that falls within the field of international relations—and that it is especially agreed that war or international misunderstandings or anything that may lead to friction or trouble is everybody's business, because it may affect the peace of the world.

16. What is the purpose of the first paragraph of the address?

a. to describe the provisions of the League of Nations in extensive detail for those persons not present at its creation
b. to establish an agreeable tone in order to unite those persons with disagreements regarding the League of Nations
c. to explain the difficult and often heated process of mapping out the League of Nations
d. to illustrate why the League of Nations is essential and how it will help resolve international disagreements

17. What effect does Wilson's recurring use of the word we have on his audience?

a. It purposely avoids mentioning any of the creators of the League of Nations by name.
b. It places blame for the League of Nations on both himself and his audience.
c. It emphasizes the creation of the League of Nations as a collective process.
d. It creates the sense that everyone involved in debating the League of Nations agreed with him.

18. Why does Wilson say, "You cannot have a representative assembly of 1.2 billion people"?

a. to illustrate the necessity of government representatives
b. to prove that large groups of people are unruly
c. to marvel at how many people will benefit from the League of Nations
d. to show how the methods of the past have failed

19. What are the Great Powers?

a. the League of Nations' abilities to represent people
b. the fourteen nations comprising the League of Nations
c. the 1.2 billion people the League of Nations represents
d. the people who first conceived of the League of Nations

20. As used in paragraph one of the excerpt, the word commission means

a. task
b. accredit
c. acquisition
d. committee

The following questions are not about a passage. Read and answer each question.

21. Which of the following statements would be LEAST relevant in a formal essay about artist Salvador Dalí?

a. Although his works are famed for their dream-like qualities, Dalí executed them with realism reminiscent of the Renaissance masters.
b. Salvador Dalí's eccentricity extended beyond his artwork, affecting the strange public persona he created, which can be witnessed in his numerous television appearances.
c. I've always found Dalí's painting *The Persistence of Memory* to be really disturbing for some reason.
d. Although Salvador Dalí is best known for his paintings, he also was active in cinema and collaborated with such filmmakers as Luis Bunuel and Alfred Hitchcock.

22. Which of the following statements would be the LEAST effective in an argument in favor of establishing a neighborhood watch organization?

a. Statistics prove that crime has risen in this neighborhood by thirty percent throughout the past five years.
b. It is impossible to trust anybody these days, but a neighborhood watch organization might help me to feel more comfortable.
c. Watch organizations have been proven to create a stronger sense of community in a neighborhood.
d. Organization meetings can help members understand their neighbors' routines so they can recognize when something out of the ordinary happens.

23. Which of the following statements describes a benefit of including headings in an informative article?

a. Headings make articles more entertaining and interesting to read by changing up the presentation.
b. Headings help stretch relatively short articles to a more substantial length.
c. Headings create the sense that the writer is particularly knowledgeable about the subject discussed in the article.
d. Headings help organize an article by making information easier to locate and clarifying the main ideas of each section.

24. Which of the following statements BEST explains the process of notating music to persons unfamiliar with this process?

a. Notating music is like math, in that both concepts involve mapping out ideas by counting.
b. Notating music involves notation on a G or C clef, depending on the instrument for which you are composing.
c. Notating music is accomplished after intense and serious musical studies.
d. Notating music involves writing down notes on staff paper for musicians to follow.

25. Which of the following statements offers the BEST conclusion to a narrative about a woman who learns to ride a horse?

a. The experience proved that even the most daunting challenges can be mastered when met with commitment, patience, and love.
b. In the end I learned how to ride a horse.
c. After I learned how to ride a horse, I decided I would next learn how to fly an airplane, which is something I've always wanted to do.
d. Horses are not only fun to ride, but they make wonderful companions.

26. Which of the following statements BEST cites a source in an essay?

a. According to historian Gertrude Blankenship, "Edgar Alan Poe's troubled childhood has a major impact on the works he would write as an adult" (Blankenship 172).
b. "Edgar Alan Poe's troubled childhood has a major impact on the works he would write as an adult" (Gertrude 172).
c. According to historian Gertrude Blankenship, "Edgar Alan Poe's troubled childhood has a major impact on the works he would write as an adult" (172).
d. "Edgar Alan Poe's troubled childhood has a major impact on the works he would write as an adult."

27. Which of the following works would be relevant in an essay exploring the topic of "man versus nature in American literature"?

a. The Sound and the Fury
b. To the Lighthouse
c. Animal Farm
d. Moby Dick

28. Which of the following speeches would be relevant in an essay exploring Civil Rights in America?

a. President John F. Kennedy's "Ich bin ein Berliner"
b. Dr. Martin Luther King, Jr.'s "I Have a Dream"
c. President Ronald Reagan's "A Time for Choosing"
d. General Douglas MacArthur's "Duty, Honor, Country"

29. Read the sentences, and then answer the question that follows.

In the past, television has been criticized as a medium without the complexity and artfulness of cinema. *Contemporary programs, such as* Mad Men, *are widely celebrated* for their intricately structured narratives and beautifully realized design.

Which of the following statements best links these sentences?

a. Today's television shows prove that the medium has not changed much.
b. *Mad Men* is a television show about the advertising business of the 1960s.
c. This attitude has changed drastically over time.
d. Television now offers a wide range of comedies, dramas, and reality shows.

30. Which of the following choices is most essential to an argument against cutting college financial aid programs?

a. statistics proving the high cost of a college education
b. a list of jobs students could perform while attending school
c. a personal story about filling out financial aid forms
d. quotations from students who have applied for financial aid

31. Which of the following statements would BEST conclude an essay about Oprah Winfrey?

a. Having conquered television, film, print, and the Internet, Oprah Winfrey has proved once and for all that she is the true queen of media.
b. There never has been another person like Oprah Winfrey, and there probably will never be one again.
c. The final episode of "The Oprah Winfrey Show" aired on May 25, 2011.
d. Oprah Winfrey first gained national fame as the host of her own long-running television talk show.

32. Which of the following sentences is MOST vivid?

a. The cat screeched loudly outside my house last night.
b. The cat's piercing cry shattered the night's drowsy stillness.
c. The cat cried louder than a dog's bark.
d. The cat made a lot of noise, and it was very disturbing.

33. Which of the following would be the LEAST successful introduction to a young adult novel?

a. Grace was always distinguished by her curiosity and cunning.
b. I was already peering out the living room window when the car first pulled into our driveway.
c. Marisol and Hector shuffled together through the newly fallen snow.
d. Candace gesticulated tempestuously as the bus left her forsaken on the curb.

34. Which of the following choices is the BEST way to become a disciplined writer?

a. Force yourself to complete a long work over a single weekend.
b. Study the works of writers you admire.
c. Set aside an hour or two to write every day.
d. Make sure to always write in total silence.

35. Read the following introduction from an essay about automobiles.

A valuable tool for crossing long distances the automobile is a friend, and perpetrator of toxic pollution, the automobile is a foe.

What is the MOST effective revision of this introduction?

a. The automobile crosses long distances, which is a good thing, but it is also a perpetrator of toxic pollution, which is bad.
b. Both a valuable tool for crossing long distances and a perpetrator of toxic pollution, the automobile is both friend and foe.
c. Automobiles are good because they help us cross long distances, but they are bad because they create a lot of pollution.
d. Both a valuable tool for crossing long distances— the automobile is both friend and foe— and perpetrator of toxic pollution.

36. Which of the following sentences would BEST build suspense in a narrative?

a. The unexpected creak of floorboards outside his room sent Andrew's heart racing.
b. Andrew awoke in the middle of the night after experiencing a terrible nightmare.
c. Andrew made sure his front door was locked every night before going to bed.
d. The dog curled up in bed next to Andrew just as it did every night.

37. Which of the following sentences would be the BEST statement to include in a speech intended to convince its audience to invest in a community theater?

a. A lot of communities do not have their own theaters, so ours would be more unique if it had one.
b. Establishing a theater is a proven way to strengthen and build revenue for its surrounding community.
c. I bet that every community that has ever had its own theater benefitted from it financially.
d. Community theaters are really good for the communities they are in.

38. In what way might the use of music enhance a presentation?

a. Music has a strong effect on the emotions, and using the right piece might help sway your audience to respond to a presentation positively.
b. People always lose interest in presentations after a while, and music is a good way to keep their attention.
c. Audiences usually enjoy listening to music more than they like to listen to people talk.
d. It is a good way to fill out a poorly organized presentation that needs to be stretched to a certain length.

39. Read the following line from a speech arguing in favor of a road repair.

Repairing Route 211 will save members of this community a lot of money.

Which of the following is the BEST follow-up statement?

a. Also the potholes that run the entire length of route 211 are unpleasant to look at.
b. Another road that requires a great deal of attention in this community is Central Highway.
c. Last year, local drivers spent over $16,000 to repair damages caused by potholes in the road.
d. During economically uncertain times, financial matters are at the forefront of all Americans' concerns.

40. Which of the following is the LEAST effective line in a formal argument about adding an Egyptian wing to a museum?

a. Public interest in Egyptian artifacts may entice more visitors, thereby generating more revenue for the museum.
b. The museum's ever-growing influx of Egyptian artifacts makes an Egyptian wing particularly necessary.
c. The revenue surplus the museum has enjoyed throughout the past few years means it already has the funding for a new Egyptian wing.
d. I think people love to look at old mummies and stuff like that, and those are the kind of things we could have in our Egyptian wing.

41. Which of the following statements represents the BEST way to evaluate the information in a source?

a. Make an educated guess about the source's accuracy.
b. Assume any printed source is completely accurate.
c. Get in touch with the person who wrote the source.
d. Check it against information in one or more other sources.

42. Which of the following statements is the BEST way to resolve a new question that arises toward the end of an oral research project?

a. Conduct further research in the hopes of answering the question.
b. Ignore the question, as it may not be relevant to the project.
c. Assume the audience will not think to ask the question.
d. Make an informed guess to answer the question.

43. While researching an oral presentation, it is MOST important to ask questions that

a. substantiate initial assumptions
b. evaluate the argument's reasoning
c. narrow the focus of the presentation
d. are grammatically correct

44. Why is remaining civil important during even the most heated debates?

a. The most mature argument inevitably will win the debate.
b. Straying from civility will lead to immediate disqualification.
c. Resorting to insults may damage the debater's credibility.
d. Uncivil actions will not appeal to the audience's emotions.

45. Which of the following steps is the MOST essential in preparing for a debate?

a. Practice your argument in front of the mirror.
b. Conduct all necessary research.
c. Introduce yourself to your opponent.
d. Get a good night's sleep.

46. Which version of the sentence is written correctly?

a. A Los-Angeles-area homeowner decided to relocate to San Francisco.
b. A Los Angeles area homeowner decided to relocate to San Francisco.
c. A Los Angeles-area homeowner decided to relocate to San Francisco.
d. A Los-Angeles-area-homeowner decided to relocate to San Francisco.

47. Which version of the sentence is written correctly?

a. Please lie the porcelain vase down gently to avoid chipping it.
b. Please lain the porcelain vase down gently to avoid chipping it.
c. Please lies the porcelain vase down gently to avoid chipping it.
d. Please lay the porcelain vase down gently to avoid chipping it.

48. As used in the sentence, "The beach is at its most placid at sunset, after most people have gone home," what does the word placid mean?

a. peaceful
b. pitiful
c. pretty
d. picturesque

49. Which version of the sentence does NOT contain any misspelled words?

a. The pompouse man thought he was better than everyone else.
b. The pompous man thought he was better than everyone else.
c. The pompus man thought he was better than everyone else.
d. The pompis man thought he was better than everyone else.

50. Taking care of the needs of others through charity and generosity is

a. philosophy.
b. physiology.
c. philanthropy.
d. philology.

51. Which version of the sentence creates the best feeling of suspense?

a. The owl pounced on the rabbit suddenly when it spied the helpless animal emerging from the brush.
b. When the owl spied the rabbit emerging from the brush, it pounced on the helpless animal suddenly.
c. The owl pounced on the helpless animal suddenly when the owl spied the rabbit emerging from the brush.
d. Suddenly, the owl pounced on the rabbit when it spied the helpless animal emerging from the brush.

52. Which of the following choices is the best way to write the sentence?

a. There instantly is no way to learn a new language.
b. Instantly there is no way to learn a new language.
c. There is no instantly way to learn a new language.
d. There is no way to learn a new language instantly.

53. Which is the best way to write the sentence?

a. What will you do with all of the vacation days you have accumulated?
b. What shall you do with all of the vacation days you have accumulated?
c. What would you do with all of the vacation days you have accumulated?
d. What may you do with all of the vacation days you have accumulated?

54. Although the street could not be seen through the translucent curtains, sunshine still flowed through them.

Based on how it is used in the sentence, the word translucent means

a. flimsy
b. transitory
c. semi-transparent
d. opaque

55. If someone were to say, "That dog is the size of a house," he or she likely would mean

a. The house is probably a doghouse.
b. The dog is literally the same size as a house.
c. The dog can be measured in yards.
d. The dog is exceptionally large.

56. Which version of the sentence is written correctly?

a. Veronica was contemptible of the noisy construction workers who made it hard to concentrate on her work.
b. Veronica was contemptuous of the noisy construction workers who made it hard to concentrate on her work.
c. Veronica was contempt of the noisy construction workers who made it hard to concentrate on her work.
d. Veronica was contemptful of the noisy construction workers who made it hard to concentrate on her work.

57. Which version of the sentence does NOT contain any misspelled words?

a. I gave my condolences to Juan, whose dog recently ran away from home.
b. I gave my condolances to Juan, whose dog recently ran away from home.
c. I gave my condolenses to Juan, whose dog recently ran away from home.
d. I gave my condolanses to Juan, whose dog recently ran away from home.

58. According to Merriam-Webster's Dictionary, which word derives from the English word fawney, which referred to a gilded brass ring?

a. fawning
b. phone
c. phony
d. fallen

Answers and Explanations

1. D: With its grotesque carvings, excessive slants, and thorny vegetation, Wuthering Heights is a strange and foreboding house. As such, the author's description contributes to the story's strange and foreboding tone. Although Mr. Lockwood seems to like the house, its description alone does not explain why he likes it. Furthermore, although a misanthrope might live in a foreboding house, this fact alone does not prove Heathcliff's misanthropy.

2. B: Although this excerpt is not overly comedic, the narrator, Mr. Lockwood, makes a few sarcastic remarks. Sarcasm combines harshness and humor. When Lockwood remarks that Joseph is sour that he "must have need of divine aid to digest his dinner," he does not mean that Joseph literally needs God's help to digest. Instead, he is making a sarcastic joke about Joseph's sourness.

3. D: Mr. Lockwood describes the ventilation as bracing. Ventilation allows the flow of cool, fresh air, which can create an invigorating sensation. Although the word bracing can mean, "supporting," "bracketing," and "staying," this is not how the author uses the word in paragraph 8.

4. C: Heathcliff seems to have little regard for his old home. He does not garden and does not have a gardening staff. As a result, the vegetation on his property will be trimmed and landscaped only if his cattle decide to nibble it. Although the statement is somewhat humorous and possibly eccentric, it does not provide evidence that Heathcliff is mad.

5. A: During the 1800s, critics were less inclined to appreciate unlikable characters. The three characters introduced in this excerpt may fit that description for many readers. Heathcliff is described as a misanthrope, or someone who hates people. Joseph is sour, which means he always seems displeased. Mr. Lockwood seems to take great pleasure in the disagreeability of these characters, as well as the house, Wuthering Heights. Critics found these qualities off-putting when Emily Bronte's novel was published in 1847.

6. B: Theseus explicitly asks Hippolyta to come with him, and he tells Demetrius and Egeus that he has "some business against our nuptial" to discuss with them. Although this scene establishes the love between Lysander and Hermia, which likely will be discussed as the scene proceeds, the reader cannot know this for certain from this excerpt.

7. D: In his second block of dialog in the excerpt, Egeus accuses Lysander of doing several things to win his daughter Hermia's love. Egeus says that Lysander "interchanged love-tokens with my child," which means Lysander gave her gifts. He says that Lysander sang to her by moonlight and had "given her rhymes," which refers to poetry. Lysander did paint her portrait.

8. C: Lysander is in love with Hermia and wants to marry her, but she is supposed to marry Demetrius. However, Lysander and Theseus reveal that Demetrius actually loves a woman named Helena. Because they are already romantically involved with the men, Helena clearly knows Demetrius loves her, and Hermia knows Lysander loves her. Although Egeus wants to keep these couples apart for his own selfish reasons, there is no reason to believe the couples are not right for each other.

9. A: Hermia's father, Egeus, is powerful, and he demands that she marry Demetrius. She realizes that her failure to marry Demetrius will bring about negative consequences, and she reveals this knowledge by saying she knows "The worst that may befall me in this case, / If I refuse to wed Demetrius." These lines imply a high cost if she refuses to marry Demetrius and continues to pursue her relationship with Lysander.

10. C: The Scarlett Letter concerns an adulterous relationship. Hermia is not yet married to Demetrious, so her relationship with Lysander is not adulterous. Since Hermia is supposed to marry Demetrious, it is not true that she is only involved with Lysander, even though he is the only man she loves. Hermia's father, Egeus, wants to keep her and Lysander apart, not she and Demetrious, whom he wants her to marry.

11. B: Article III states, "Congress shall make no law respecting an establishment of religion." Not using government to enforce the establishment of a single religion is one way to maintain a separation of church (religion) and state (government). Although the Article defends the right of people to assemble peaceably, it does not encourage such activities outright. The Article refers to grievances against the government but does not list them, nor does it mention anything about harmful speech.

12. D: Article V protects homeowners and the privacy of their homes by stating that soldiers may not be quartered, or live, in their homes without the homeowners consent. Article IV protects the right to own weapons, but it does not make any mention of privacy.

13. A: Articles VI through XI all deal with protecting the property and rights of those accused of committing a crime. These articles ensure the accused are not subjected to unfair searches or arrests and entitled to a fair trial before a grand jury. The other answer choices do not address everything that Articles VI through XI entail. None of these articles deal with the protection of victims of violent crimes.

14. D: The best way to validate the information in a document is to consult the original versions, and original copies of it can be viewed in the National Archives and the New York Public Library. Books and people have been known to make mistakes. Photos on the Internet are easily manipulated, so they may not always be reliable.

15. C: James Madison made the Bill of Rights clear and easy to understand by organizing it in short sections devoted to each of its thirteen articles. It is not arranged in order of importance, and its organization does not suggest any articles are more important than others. Fluid prose is not the purpose of this government document.

16. B: Wilson opens his address by acknowledging that some disagreement emerged during the process of creating the League of Nations, but he does not depict these disagreements as heated or angry. Rather, he emphasizes positive words, such as constructive and encouraging. Such terms help establish a peaceful, agreeable tone designed to congratulate and unite persons who had disagreements while creating the League of Nations.

17. C: Wilson's use of the pronoun we united himself and his audience, emphasizing that while he was a leading proponent of the League of Nations, its establishment occurred by way of a collective process. Wilson begins his address by stating that not everyone involved agreed on every issue, which means that some people disagreed with him on certain matters. Nothing in this passage suggests Wilson purposely avoiding mention of any of the League's co-creators by name, nor would he "blame" anyone for helping to create a league of which he was in favor.

18. A: Wilson intended the image of 1.2 billion representatives in a single assembly as somewhat absurd, thereby illustrating the necessity of a much smaller assembly of government representatives. While a group of 1.2 billion people likely would be unruly, this characteristic is not the purpose of Wilson's comment, nor was his purpose to marvel at the great number of people the League of Nations would represent.

19. B: In paragraph four of this excerpt, Wilson says, "Fourteen nations were represented, among them all of those powers which for convenience we have called the Great Powers, and among the rest a representation of the greatest variety of circumstances and interests."

20. D: In paragraph one, Wilson says, "It gives me pleasure to add to this formal reading of the result of our labors that the character of the discussion, which occurred at the sittings of the commission was not only of the most constructive but of the most encouraging sort." In this context, commission means a group working together to accomplish a goal, in this case, the establishment of the League of Nations. Although commission can be used to mean "task," "accredit," and "acquisition," paragraph one of the excerpt does not use the word any of these ways.

21. C: Use of the first-person point of view and a reliance on personal opinion creates an informal tone. A formal essay should be written in the third-person and rely on assertions supported by research rather than upon vague personal opinions.

22. B: This sentence makes a broad, overly subjective statement. One of the keys to establishing an effective argument involves presenting information formally and objectively, so it cannot be dismissed as mere personal opinion. The other answer choices accomplish this task well.

23. D: Headings should summarize briefly the main idea of a section. They stand out from the text that follows, usually by being bolded and offset. These characteristics make headings easy to spot. As a result, the sections also are easier to locate. Although headings do indeed change up the presentation of an article, this characteristic hardly represents their main benefit.

24. A: This sentence uses a concept familiar to most people (math) to explain a concept that might seem complex to persons who never have tried doing it (notating music). Technical terms, such as "G and C clef" do not make the concept any easier to grasp. Explaining that the ability to notate music comes with study does not give any indication how to accomplish the actual notation. Choice D explains notation, but gives no indication of how to accomplish the task.

25. A: A strong conclusion briefly reflects on the experience discussed in the narrative while also indicating the experience's resolution. This conclusion accomplishes these characteristics by reflecting on the difficult process of learning to ride a horse ("the most daunting challenges") and how it was resolved ("with commitment, patience, and love"). Simply saying, "In the end I learned how to ride a horse," states the conclusion of the experience clearly, but it provides no summarization or insight into all that experience entailed.

26. C: Citation is important because it provides credit to the original authors of quotations used in others' writing. Citations must include the last name of the author being cited (in this case, Blankenship) and the page of the source upon which the quotation originally appeared (172). Citing the author's name twice is redundant and incorrect.

27. D: Herman Melville's 1851 novel Moby Dick is a cornerstone of American literature. The novel is about a sea captain's hunt for the white whale that severed his leg. This essential exploration of the theme of "man versus nature" is one of the most read and studied novels in American literature.

28. B: The American Civil Rights movement of the 1960s sought equal rights for Americans of all races. The definitive speech of the movement is "I Have a Dream" by its leader, Dr. Martin Luther King, Jr. Any thorough discussion of the Civil Rights movement should reference this speech, which maps out a future in which people of all races can come together in total harmony.

29. C: The first sentence explains how television once was criticized. The second sentence shows how contemporary shows now are being praised. They require a linking sentence indicating that an attitude change toward television has occurred over time. Explaining the premise of *Mad Men* or the variety of shows on television does not address the best way to link these sentences. Stating, "Today's television shows prove that the medium has not changed much," contradicts the second sentence.

30. A: An argument is best supported with solid, factual evidence. The purpose of financial aid programs is to help pay for the educations of students who otherwise could not afford to attend college without aid. The best way to prove these programs are necessary is to provide solid evidence that college education is too expensive for many potential students. Such statistics would show that many people would not be able to obtain a college education without financial aid from the government.

31. A: A strong concluding statement reminds the reader of all that precedes it while making a brief, final observation about the topic. This statement lists all that Oprah Winfrey accomplished (she "conquered television, film, print, and the Internet") and concludes, "she is the true queen of media." The other answer choices either provide random details or vague personal opinions about her.

32. B: Vivid, descriptive language helps a narrative come to life, accomplished here with strong and interesting adjectives (piercing), verbs (shattered), and figurative language (the night's drowsy stillness). Simply stating the facts ("The cat made a lot of noise, and it was very disturbing") or using lazy comparisons ("The cat cried louder than a dog's bark") does not create a particularly vivid picture of the action in a narrative.

33. D: Writers of young adult novels should not to patronize their readers with overly simple language, but they also need to be careful that their vocabulary is age appropriate. Readers of young adult novels may be as young as 14-years old, and words such as "gesticulated," "tempestuously," and "forsaken" might be beyond their comprehension. The other introductions are much clearer for their intended audiences.

34. C: Disciplined writing comes with a steady writing routine. By setting aside an hour or two to write every day, the process eventually should become routine. Forcing yourself into long periods of writing may only create frustration. Studying the works of writers you admire may make you a better writer, but it won't make you a more disciplined one. Some people find listening to music to be inspirational while they write, so working in total silence may not necessarily make you a more disciplined writer.

35. B: This is the most effective revision. The syntax is clearer than the original sentence and it retains the vivid description of automobile as a "friend and foe." The other choices either are poorly structured or are missing the figurative language of the original.

36. A: Suspense is created with the suggestion of major details yet to come. This sentence creates suspense by implying danger (a mysterious someone or something is creaking on floorboards outside Andrew's room) while not yet revealing what is happening. The reader now wants to know who or what is creeping outside of Andrew's room. The other answer choices do not produce this same effect.

37. B: Potential investors would expect a confident, formal speech presented with details relevant to financial matters. The other answer choices stray off this point, make broad unsupported claims, or are too informal for the given audience.

38. A: Music does have a strong effect on human emotions and can be used to heighten points in a speech. For example, sad music played over scenes of social injustice may help sway the audience to understand the issue on a deeper level than might a mere discussion. The right audience may respond powerfully to a presentation enhanced with music. Whether or not audiences prefer to listen to music rather than an oral presentation has no bearing on whether or not using music in a presentation is appropriate. Avoid overly broad statements such as "people always lose interest in presentations."

39. C: The first statement establishes the idea that repairing Route 211 will have financial consequences for the community. The correct answer choice supports this statement by providing specific figures regarding the amount of money the potholes in Route 211 cost drivers last year. The other answer choices may be relevant in the argument, but they do not follow the statement in the question as well.

40. D: Strong statements stated clearly are keys to a strong argument. This statement is neither strong nor clear. It contains an unsupported generalization ("I think people love to look at old mummies") and the word choice and syntax are also sloppy and informal. The other answer choices are formal and convincing arguments in favor of the creation of an Egyptian wing.

41. D: Even printed sources can contain mistakes or outdated information. The best way to evaluate the accuracy of the information in a particular source is to check it against discussions of the same topic in other sources. The information that appears in the most sources likely will be the most accurate.

42. A: A thorough discussion of any topic should address all questions as thoroughly as possible. Even if you assume you have come to the end of the research portion of your project, it still is important to answer all new questions that may arise with further research. Hoping the audience won't think to ask the question or guessing about its answer may only weaken the central argument of your project.

43. B: First assumptions are not always correct. Always question the reasoning of your central arguments when researching an oral presentation. Be flexible enough to revise or even completely rebuild your argument based on the answers to new questions that might arise while researching it.

44. C: A composed, professional demeanor strengthens the credibility of a debater. Losing that demeanor by resorting to uncivil actions such as insults may damage that credibility. Even though uncivil actions could appeal to an audience's emotions and the most mature debater is not always the winner, remaining civil during any debate is best.

45. B: The most basic task in preparing for a debate is developing a strong argument. Strong arguments result from conducting thorough research by consulting reliable sources. Without a well-substantiated argument, there can be no debate. Practicing in front of a mirror, meeting your opponent, and getting a good night's sleep are all important, but not nearly as essential as conducting thorough research.

46. C: A compound modifier consists of two or more words, which must be linked with one or more hyphens. In this sentence, "Los Angeles-homeowner" is a compound modifier. Although "Los Angeles" consists of two words, it is a single city name and does not require a hyphen between "Los" and "Angeles."

47. D: The words lie and lay are often confused, but they are not used in the same way. Lie means to recline, as a person might lie on a bed. Lay is a verb meaning to place an object. Since a porcelain vase is an object, the correct word is lay in this sentence.

48. A: Although the words *pretty* and *picturesque* make sense in the context of this sentence, *placid* means peaceful. A beach would be most peaceful when people have left it after sunset.

49. B: The word pompous, meaning arrogant or self-important, is spelled with an "ou," creating an "uh" sound.

50. C: The root word "phil" means love, which is a feeling often at the root of charity and generosity. The pursuit of taking care of the needs of others through charity and generosity is called philanthropy. A philosophy is a system of beliefs. Physiology refers to the functions and processes of living organisms. Philology is the study of written materials.

51. B: Although all of these sentences are technically correct, only choice B uses syntax to establish a feeling of suspense. It achieves this by saving the action—the owl pouncing on the rabbit—for the end of the sentence. The other answer choices give away the action right away.

52. D: Choices B and C clearly misuse the adverb "instantly" by placing it where it does not make sense. Choice A is more of a grey area. Placing "instantly" inside the phrase "to learn" creates a split infinitive. Technically, a split infinitive is a form of incorrect grammar, yet it has become so widely used that many people now accept it as correct. However, it remains technically incorrect, and choice D is the best answer choice.

53. A: "What will you do with all of the vacation days you have accumulated?" is the correct way to write this sentence. The word "shall" in choice B is technically correct, yet it is archaic, which means it isn't generally used any more. Unless this sentence was dialogue in a story set in the past, it might sound strange. Choice C is incorrect because the word "would" suggests a desire rather than an actuality. Because the vacation days have already been accumulated, the person the speaker is addressing does not have to merely desire them.

54. C: According to the sentence, while certain things could not be seen through the curtains, light could. The curtains are not transparent enough to show the street, yet they are transparent enough to show sunshine. The prefix "semi" means "partially." Based on this context, you can conclude that translucent and semitransparent share the same meaning. Although something that is flimsy may be transparent, this is not always the case, so the words are not synonyms. Transitory shares the root word "trans," meaning "through," but it means "not lasting." Something that is opaque does not allow light to pass through it, which is the opposite of translucent.

55. D: The phrase "That dog is the size of a house" is an example of hyperbole, a form of figurative language that employs exaggeration. No dog is literally the size of a house, so one can only assume this phrase means the dog is exceptionally large. Since houses are known for being large they are good indicators of exceptional size.

56. B: Contempt is a feeling of scorn or disdain, and to be contemptuous is to experience or express that feeling. Contemptible is something that inspired contempt, which in Veronica's case, would be the noisy construction workers. Contemptful is not a real word.

57. A: The word condolences means an expression of sympathy, and only choice A spells it correctly.

58. C: A word's origin, or etymology, can sometimes be guessed by examining the word. A brass ring merely gilded with gold, a fawney, is hardly the same thing as a solid gold ring. Attempting to pass of such a ring as pure gold would be untruthful and the ring would only be a fake gold ring. The words phony and fake share the same meaning. Although fawning sounds and looks similar to fawney, the former means flattering or submissive, which provides no indication of the real meaning of fawney.

How to Overcome Test Anxiety

Just the thought of taking a test is enough to make most people a little nervous. A test is an important event that can have a long-term impact on your future, so it's important to take it seriously and it's natural to feel anxious about performing well. But just because anxiety is normal, that doesn't mean that it's helpful in test taking, or that you should simply accept it as part of your life. Anxiety can have a variety of effects. These effects can be mild, like making you feel slightly nervous, or severe, like blocking your ability to focus or remember even a simple detail.

If you experience test anxiety—whether severe or mild—it's important to know how to beat it. To discover this, first you need to understand what causes test anxiety.

Causes of Test Anxiety

While we often think of anxiety as an uncontrollable emotional state, it can actually be caused by simple, practical things. One of the most common causes of test anxiety is that a person does not feel adequately prepared for their test. This feeling can be the result of many different issues such as poor study habits or lack of organization, but the most common culprit is time management. Starting to study too late, failing to organize your study time to cover all of the material, or being distracted while you study will mean that you're not well prepared for the test. This may lead to cramming the night before, which will cause you to be physically and mentally exhausted for the test. Poor time management also contributes to feelings of stress, fear, and hopelessness as you realize you are not well prepared but don't know what to do about it.

Other times, test anxiety is not related to your preparation for the test but comes from unresolved fear. This may be a past failure on a test, or poor performance on tests in general. It may come from comparing yourself to others who seem to be performing better or from the stress of living up to expectations. Anxiety may be driven by fears of the future—how failure on this test would affect your educational and career goals. These fears are often completely irrational, but they can still negatively impact your test performance.

Elements of Test Anxiety

As mentioned earlier, test anxiety is considered to be an emotional state, but it has physical and mental components as well. Sometimes you may not even realize that you are suffering from test anxiety until you notice the physical symptoms. These can include trembling hands, rapid heartbeat, sweating, nausea, and tense muscles. Extreme anxiety may lead to fainting or vomiting. Obviously, any of these symptoms can have a negative impact on testing. It is important to recognize them as soon as they begin to occur so that you can address the problem before it damages your performance.

The mental components of test anxiety include trouble focusing and inability to remember learned information. During a test, your mind is on high alert, which can help you recall information and stay focused for an extended period of time. However, anxiety interferes with your mind's natural processes, causing you to blank out, even on the questions you know well. The strain of testing during anxiety makes it difficult to stay focused, especially on a test that may take several hours. Extreme anxiety can take a huge mental toll, making it difficult not only to recall test information but even to understand the test questions or pull your thoughts together.

Effects of Test Anxiety

Test anxiety is like a disease—if left untreated, it will get progressively worse. Anxiety leads to poor performance, and this reinforces the feelings of fear and failure, which in turn lead to poor performances on subsequent tests. It can grow from a mild nervousness to a crippling condition. If allowed to progress, test anxiety can have a big impact on your schooling, and consequently on your future.

Test anxiety can spread to other parts of your life. Anxiety on tests can become anxiety in any stressful situation, and blanking on a test can turn into panicking in a job situation. But fortunately, you don't have to let anxiety rule your testing and determine your grades. There are a number of relatively simple steps you can take to move past anxiety and function normally on a test and in the rest of life.

Physical Steps for Beating Test Anxiety

While test anxiety is a serious problem, the good news is that it can be overcome. It doesn't have to control your ability to think and remember information. While it may take time, you can begin taking steps today to beat anxiety.

Just as your first hint that you may be struggling with anxiety comes from the physical symptoms, the first step to treating it is also physical. Rest is crucial for having a clear, strong mind. If you are tired, it is much easier to give in to anxiety. But if you establish good sleep habits, your body and mind will be ready to perform optimally, without the strain of exhaustion. Additionally, sleeping well helps you to retain information better, so you're more likely to recall the answers when you see the test questions.

Getting good sleep means more than going to bed on time. It's important to allow your brain time to relax. Take study breaks from time to time so it doesn't get overworked, and don't study right before bed. Take time to rest your mind before trying to rest your body, or you may find it difficult to fall asleep.

Along with sleep, other aspects of physical health are important in preparing for a test. Good nutrition is vital for good brain function. Sugary foods and drinks may give a burst of energy but this burst is followed by a crash, both physically and emotionally. Instead, fuel your body with protein and vitamin-rich foods.

Also, drink plenty of water. Dehydration can lead to headaches and exhaustion, especially if your brain is already under stress from the rigors of the test. Particularly if your test is a long one, drink water during the breaks. And if possible, take an energy-boosting snack to eat between sections.

Along with sleep and diet, a third important part of physical health is exercise. Maintaining a steady workout schedule is helpful, but even taking 5-minute study breaks to walk can help get your blood pumping faster and clear your head. Exercise also releases endorphins, which contribute to a positive feeling and can help combat test anxiety.

When you nurture your physical health, you are also contributing to your mental health. If your body is healthy, your mind is much more likely to be healthy as well. So take time to rest, nourish your body with healthy food and water, and get moving as much as possible. Taking these physical steps will make you stronger and more able to take the mental steps necessary to overcome test anxiety.

Mental Steps for Beating Test Anxiety

Working on the mental side of test anxiety can be more challenging, but as with the physical side, there are clear steps you can take to overcome it. As mentioned earlier, test anxiety often stems from lack of preparation, so the obvious solution is to prepare for the test. Effective studying may be the most important weapon you have for beating test anxiety, but you can and should employ several other mental tools to combat fear.

First, boost your confidence by reminding yourself of past success—tests or projects that you aced. If you're putting as much effort into preparing for this test as you did for those, there's no reason you should expect to fail here. Work hard to prepare; then trust your preparation.

Second, surround yourself with encouraging people. It can be helpful to find a study group, but be sure that the people you're around will encourage a positive attitude. If you spend time with others who are anxious or cynical, this will only contribute to your own anxiety. Look for others who are motivated to study hard from a desire to succeed, not from a fear of failure.

Third, reward yourself. A test is physically and mentally tiring, even without anxiety, and it can be helpful to have something to look forward to. Plan an activity following the test, regardless of the outcome, such as going to a movie or getting ice cream.

When you are taking the test, if you find yourself beginning to feel anxious, remind yourself that you know the material. Visualize successfully completing the test. Then take a few deep, relaxing breaths and return to it. Work through the questions carefully but with confidence, knowing that you are capable of succeeding.

Developing a healthy mental approach to test taking will also aid in other areas of life. Test anxiety affects more than just the actual test—it can be damaging to your mental health and even contribute to depression. It's important to beat test anxiety before it becomes a problem for more than testing.

Study Strategy

Being prepared for the test is necessary to combat anxiety, but what does being prepared look like? You may study for hours on end and still not feel prepared. What you need is a strategy for test prep. The next few pages outline our recommended steps to help you plan out and conquer the challenge of preparation.

Step 1: Scope Out the Test

Learn everything you can about the format (multiple choice, essay, etc.) and what will be on the test. Gather any study materials, course outlines, or sample exams that may be available. Not only will this help you to prepare, but knowing what to expect can help to alleviate test anxiety.

Step 2: Map Out the Material

Look through the textbook or study guide and make note of how many chapters or sections it has. Then divide these over the time you have. For example, if a book has 15 chapters and you have five days to study, you need to cover three chapters each day. Even better, if you have the time, leave an extra day at the end for overall review after you have gone through the material in depth.

If time is limited, you may need to prioritize the material. Look through it and make note of which sections you think you already have a good grasp on, and which need review. While you are studying, skim quickly through the familiar sections and take more time on the challenging parts.

Write out your plan so you don't get lost as you go. Having a written plan also helps you feel more in control of the study, so anxiety is less likely to arise from feeling overwhelmed at the amount to cover.

STEP 3: GATHER YOUR TOOLS

Decide what study method works best for you. Do you prefer to highlight in the book as you study and then go back over the highlighted portions? Or do you type out notes of the important information? Or is it helpful to make flashcards that you can carry with you? Assemble the pens, index cards, highlighters, post-it notes, and any other materials you may need so you won't be distracted by getting up to find things while you study.

If you're having a hard time retaining the information or organizing your notes, experiment with different methods. For example, try color-coding by subject with colored pens, highlighters, or post-it notes. If you learn better by hearing, try recording yourself reading your notes so you can listen while in the car, working out, or simply sitting at your desk. Ask a friend to quiz you from your flashcards, or try teaching someone the material to solidify it in your mind.

STEP 4: CREATE YOUR ENVIRONMENT

It's important to avoid distractions while you study. This includes both the obvious distractions like visitors and the subtle distractions like an uncomfortable chair (or a too-comfortable couch that makes you want to fall asleep). Set up the best study environment possible: good lighting and a comfortable work area. If background music helps you focus, you may want to turn it on, but otherwise keep the room quiet. If you are using a computer to take notes, be sure you don't have any other windows open, especially applications like social media, games, or anything else that could distract you. Silence your phone and turn off notifications. Be sure to keep water close by so you stay hydrated while you study (but avoid unhealthy drinks and snacks).

Also, take into account the best time of day to study. Are you freshest first thing in the morning? Try to set aside some time then to work through the material. Is your mind clearer in the afternoon or evening? Schedule your study session then. Another method is to study at the same time of day that you will take the test, so that your brain gets used to working on the material at that time and will be ready to focus at test time.

STEP 5: STUDY!

Once you have done all the study preparation, it's time to settle into the actual studying. Sit down, take a few moments to settle your mind so you can focus, and begin to follow your study plan. Don't give in to distractions or let yourself procrastinate. This is your time to prepare so you'll be ready to fearlessly approach the test. Make the most of the time and stay focused.

Of course, you don't want to burn out. If you study too long you may find that you're not retaining the information very well. Take regular study breaks. For example, taking five minutes out of every hour to walk briskly, breathing deeply and swinging your arms, can help your mind stay fresh.

As you get to the end of each chapter or section, it's a good idea to do a quick review. Remind yourself of what you learned and work on any difficult parts. When you feel that you've mastered the material, move on to the next part. At the end of your study session, briefly skim through your notes again.

But while review is helpful, cramming last minute is NOT. If at all possible, work ahead so that you won't need to fit all your study into the last day. Cramming overloads your brain with more information than it can process and retain, and your tired mind may struggle to recall even previously learned information when it is overwhelmed with last-minute study. Also, the urgent nature of cramming and the stress placed on your brain contribute to anxiety. You'll be more likely to go to the test feeling unprepared and having trouble thinking clearly.

So don't cram, and don't stay up late before the test, even just to review your notes at a leisurely pace. Your brain needs rest more than it needs to go over the information again. In fact, plan to finish your studies by noon or early afternoon the day before the test. Give your brain the rest of the day to relax or focus on other things, and get a good night's sleep. Then you will be fresh for the test and better able to recall what you've studied.

Step 6: Take a Practice Test

Many courses offer sample tests, either online or in the study materials. This is an excellent resource to check whether you have mastered the material, as well as to prepare for the test format and environment.

Check the test format ahead of time: the number of questions, the type (multiple choice, free response, etc.), and the time limit. Then create a plan for working through them. For example, if you have 30 minutes to take a 60-question test, your limit is 30 seconds per question. Spend less time on the questions you know well so that you can take more time on the difficult ones.

If you have time to take several practice tests, take the first one open book, with no time limit. Work through the questions at your own pace and make sure you fully understand them. Gradually work up to taking a test under test conditions: sit at a desk with all study materials put away and set a timer. Pace yourself to make sure you finish the test with time to spare and go back to check your answers if you have time.

After each test, check your answers. On the questions you missed, be sure you understand why you missed them. Did you misread the question (tests can use tricky wording)? Did you forget the information? Or was it something you hadn't learned? Go back and study any shaky areas that the practice tests reveal.

Taking these tests not only helps with your grade, but also aids in combating test anxiety. If you're already used to the test conditions, you're less likely to worry about it, and working through tests until you're scoring well gives you a confidence boost. Go through the practice tests until you feel comfortable, and then you can go into the test knowing that you're ready for it.

Test Tips

On test day, you should be confident, knowing that you've prepared well and are ready to answer the questions. But aside from preparation, there are several test day strategies you can employ to maximize your performance.

First, as stated before, get a good night's sleep the night before the test (and for several nights before that, if possible). Go into the test with a fresh, alert mind rather than staying up late to study.

Try not to change too much about your normal routine on the day of the test. It's important to eat a nutritious breakfast, but if you normally don't eat breakfast at all, consider eating just a protein bar. If you're a coffee drinker, go ahead and have your normal coffee. Just make sure you time it so that the caffeine doesn't wear off right in the middle of your test. Avoid sugary beverages, and drink enough water to stay hydrated but not so much that you need a restroom break 10 minutes into the test. If your test isn't first thing in the morning, consider going for a walk or doing a light workout before the test to get your blood flowing.

Allow yourself enough time to get ready, and leave for the test with plenty of time to spare so you won't have the anxiety of scrambling to arrive in time. Another reason to be early is to select a good seat. It's helpful to sit away from doors and windows, which can be distracting. Find a good seat, get out your supplies, and settle your mind before the test begins.

When the test begins, start by going over the instructions carefully, even if you already know what to expect. Make sure you avoid any careless mistakes by following the directions.

Then begin working through the questions, pacing yourself as you've practiced. If you're not sure on an answer, don't spend too much time on it, and don't let it shake your confidence. Either skip it and come back later, or eliminate as many wrong answers as possible and guess among the remaining ones. Don't dwell on these questions as you continue—put them out of your mind and focus on what lies ahead.

Be sure to read all of the answer choices, even if you're sure the first one is the right answer. Sometimes you'll find a better one if you keep reading. But don't second-guess yourself if you do immediately know the answer. Your gut instinct is usually right. Don't let test anxiety rob you of the information you know.

If you have time at the end of the test (and if the test format allows), go back and review your answers. Be cautious about changing any, since your first instinct tends to be correct, but make sure you didn't misread any of the questions or accidentally mark the wrong answer choice. Look over any you skipped and make an educated guess.

At the end, leave the test feeling confident. You've done your best, so don't waste time worrying about your performance or wishing you could change anything. Instead, celebrate the successful completion of this test. And finally, use this test to learn how to deal with anxiety even better next time.

Review Video: Test Anxiety
Visit mometrix.com/academy and enter code: 100340

Important Qualification

Not all anxiety is created equal. If your test anxiety is causing major issues in your life beyond the classroom or testing center, or if you are experiencing troubling physical symptoms related to your anxiety, it may be a sign of a serious physiological or psychological condition. If this sounds like your situation, we strongly encourage you to seek professional help.

Thank You

We at Mometrix would like to extend our heartfelt thanks to you, our friend and patron, for allowing us to play a part in your journey. It is a privilege to serve people from all walks of life who are unified in their commitment to building the best future they can for themselves.

The preparation you devote to these important testing milestones may be the most valuable educational opportunity you have for making a real difference in your life. We encourage you to put your heart into it—that feeling of succeeding, overcoming, and yes, conquering will be well worth the hours you've invested.

We want to hear your story, your struggles and your successes, and if you see any opportunities for us to improve our materials so we can help others even more effectively in the future, please share that with us as well. **The team at Mometrix would be absolutely thrilled to hear from you!** So please, send us an email (support@mometrix.com) and let's stay in touch.

If you'd like some additional help, check out these other resources we offer for your exam:

http://MometrixFlashcards.com/MCA

Online Resources

Due to our efforts to try to keep this book to a manageable length, we've created a link that will give you access to all of your online resources:

mometrix.com/resources719/ssmcag10read

It's Your Moment, Let's Celebrate It!

Share your story @mometrixtestpreparation